AF579983

SHOTGUNS AND SHOOTING

The four principal forms of the modern shotgun (*top to bottom*): side-by-side double, over-and-under, pump action and semi-automatic.

SHOTGUNS AND SHOOTING

by

E. S. McCAWLEY, Jr.

VNR VAN NOSTRAND REINHOLD COMPANY
NEW YORK CINCINNATI TORONTO LONDON MELBOURNE

Van Nostrand Reinhold Company Regional Offices:
New York Cincinnati Chicago Millbrae Dallas

Van Nostrand Reinhold Company International Offices:
London Toronto Melbourne

Library of Congress Catalog Card Number 65-26469

ISBN 0-442-25221-8

Published by Van Nostrand Reinhold Company
A Division of Litton Educational Publishing, Inc.
450 West 33rd Street, New York, N.Y. 10001

3 5 7 9 11 13 15 16 14 12 10 8 6 4 2

Credit is given to Science and Mechanics Publishing Company for permission to use material from the author‘s *OPEN SEASON ON CLAY PIGEONS* originally published in Gun Handbook's Shooting Guide; and to GUNSPORT MAGAZINE for permission to use material from the author's *HOW TO HIT FLYING TARGETS* which originally appeared in their July 1964 issue; to Dan Holland for illustration #40; to David O. Moreton for #'s 14, 15, 16, 17; to J. P. Linduska for #'s 41 and 42; to Ducks Unlimited, #33; to the Winchester News Bureau for #'s 4, 5, 6, and 7; to NSSF for #'s 27, 28, 29, 36, and 38; to the USDA for #'s 1 and 35; and to the Bureau of Reclamation, U. S. Department of the Interior for #2.

Contents

List of Illustrations

CHAPTER 1

The Fun of Shotgun Shooting

It was a bone-chilling morning in mid-November. Here and there, in the marsh, a gossamer thin coat of ice covered the shallowest water. In the east an anemic sun edged its way skyward, defying a scanty cover of high clouds.

Two men crouched in a duck blind at the edge of the swamp, their eyes searching and their ears tuned to the highest frequency. A Labrador retriever waited next to them, his tail thumping the ground in occasional expectation. A spread of decoys, artfully anchored in the posture of feeding birds, covered the water in front of them. Guns loaded and duck calls at the ready, the hunters waited for whatever might come.

Suddenly a flight of four mallards appeared over the trees, flying out of the sun across the marsh. Raising the calls to their lips, the hunters started "talking mallard." The birds flew on heedless and then, almost as an afterthought, turned and came in towards the spread of decoys.

The hunters kept their calls talking until the birds were within range. Then, as though by a prearranged signal, they jumped to their feet and fired. The ducks flared off untouched. Shaking their heads in disbelief, the two men settled back in the blind to await the next chance.

This scene might just as easily have been a frosty corn field with the hunters following a pointer in search of pheasants, a palmetto field with quail the quarry, or any number of other situations in upland or waterfowl hunting.

For the uninitiated, it is sometimes hard to fathom the reason why men (and to an increasing extent women) will travel vast distances, walk miles, and often undergo actual physical discomfort (those duck hunters were cold, in spite of their long woolies) in pursuit of their favorite type of scatter-gunning sport. The answer, however, is simple: shotgun shooting and hunting with a shotgun are fun!

The pleasures these sports give comes not just from mastering the skill of hitting a flying target with a charge of shot but, to an equal degree, from being in the out-of-doors and learning to fathom the ways of game birds and animals in the company of congenial companions.

Throughout history, man has been concerned with the subject of hunting. To our forebears, the problem was one of necessity. Supermarkets were scarce and meat had to be found in the wild. As the human race became more sophisticated and civilized, hunting evolved from a matter of need to one of sport. Today, more than 15,000,000 hunting licenses are sold in this country every year and there are more than 20,000,000 people who hunt and shoot. The additional 5-odd million hunt under conditions that do not require a license, or they are target shooters.

No one is exactly sure just how many of these people are shotgun enthusiasts, but a recent survey, made by the Fish and Wildlife Service of the Department of the Interior, indicates that there are 6,000,000 duck hunters and 12,000,000 upland game hunters. Of course, there are many people who hunt both types of game.

Numerous others either sharpen their eyes in "batting practice" at clay target shooting or are serious competitors in the organized clay target sports of trap and skeet.

This whole group of sportsmen share the fun and challenge of mastering the art of handling a shotgun, whether in the fields or at the traps.

Types of Shotgun Shooting

As we have indicated, there are three main types of shotgun shooting: upland hunting, waterfowl hunting, and the clay target sports. Detailed data will be presented in later chapters. For now, however, let's take a brief look at each.

Upland hunting includes the pursuit of birds such as quail, grouse, pheasants, partridge, doves, woodcock, turkeys and animals such as squirrels, rabbits, and even bear and deer. As the name implies, it is done primarily in country away from bodies of water.

Waterfowl hunting is concerned with water and shore birds such as ducks, geese, and rail. As opposed to upland hunting, it is done largely over water, ranging from the farm ponds and marshes, frequented by the dabbling ducks, to the large

Upland hunters with their dog

Waterfowl shooting from a blind

Shooters on a skeet field

bodies of salt and fresh water, favored by the sea ducks, broadbills, red heads and canvasbacks.

The clay target sports include trap shooting, skeet shooting and a number of less formal inanimate shooting games where a small circular disk of clay and pitch, propelled by a spring actuated device known as a trap, is the quarry.

To an increasing degree, shotguns firing rifled slug loads or buckshot, are being used to hunt animals up to and including white tail deer or black bear in size. Local regulations, in many areas that are becoming increasingly heavily populated, require the use of these combinations for safety reasons. As we will see later, the smooth bore gun, with these loads, is extremely effective at ranges of less than 100 yards.

Basically, the shotgun is designed for short range use at flying or moving targets. Of all sporting firearms, it is truly most deserving of the term, "Sporting." As any scattergunner will readily testify, there are days when the game really seems to have the upper hand, in spite of the fact that a full choke gun can put better than 70 percent of the shot pattern, of any size shot, in a 30 inch circle at 40 yards.

The sporting part of the game of shotgun shooting comes from the fact that the quarry, be it a live bird or a clay target, moves at speeds of up to 50 or more miles an hour. With the exception of deer or bear hunting with a shotgun, no true sportsman would ever dream of shooting a bird sitting in a tree, on the ground or on the water. The targets must be moving in order to make the game sport. In the process of moving, at the speeds involved, the game has at least an equal chance. Even the most experienced scatter gunner has had days when he felt he couldn't hit the side of a barn.

Truly, shotgun shooting and hunting has a heritage as one of the oldest and finest of the shooting sports. In the chapters that follow, we'll try to trace the how's and why's of this rich tradition and we'll try to tell you something about the sport today.

CHAPTER 2

How It All Began

On that prehistoric day when a cave man hurled a rock at a bird or animal he wanted to take home for his dinner, he invented the first missile. From that time on, man has been concerned with the problem of improving the range, accuracy and knockdown power of projectiles. In the process, successive weapons, ranging from the earliest spears and bows and arrows to the latest intercontinental rockets, have been developed.

Each step, in this evolutionary process, has resulted in a device more lethal than the last. As is true of most inventions throughout the history of man, the progression in weapons design has been mothered by need. Wild creatures, increasingly aware of danger from man, learned to stay out of range of hand thrown rocks, which led to the introduction of the more accurate sling shot and bow and arrow. Then human enemies of man developed better defenses such as shields, fortifications and armor, leading to the development of crossbows and other more complex devices.

The pace of progress towards more sophisticated arms was not constant, however, The development of weapons, actuated either mechanically or by the strength of the human arm, reached a high point in the days of the Roman Empire. With the fall of Rome and the decline of civilization in feudal Europe, progress stopped. At the end of the 13th Century, the weapons of war and sport were not very different from those in use a thousand years earlier.

The Introduction of Gunpowder

Sometime in the 14th Century, or perhaps just prior to it, men started using gunpowder to propel projectiles. This signaled a revolution and an era of progress in weapons development unparalleled in history until the start of the atomic age.

In spite of his magnificent artistic, architectural and engineering achievements, Renaissance man was not noted for his record keeping talents. As a result, no one is sure about the exact origins of gun powder. Legend has it that knowledge of the substance found its way to Europe from the Orient via the Near East. All that we know for sure is that Roger Bacon, the renowned English friar who lived from 1214 to 1294, was the first European to record its existence.

Whatever the details of the origin of gunpowder may be, we know that Roger Bacon's formula resulted in a highly combustible substance. When burned in open air, the compound produced a sudden flash of fire. Ignited in a confined place, it resulted in an explosion, caused by rapidly expanding gases seeking some means of escape.

The First Firearms

At first, this new development was something of a laboratory curiosity. While no one is sure who first conceived the idea of using it as a force to propel a projectile, it is likely that the notion occurred to a number of different people at roughly the same time. We do know that the first primitive guns appeared in Spain at about the period that Friar Bacon recorded his experiments. These early weapons, known as firepots, were little more than iron buckets which were loaded with powder and then rocks. The powder was ignited by touching red hot coals to a hole at the base of the bucket.

Since the inventors of these devices had little knowledge of metallurgy or the stress forces created by the resulting explosion, the gunners probably ran almost as great a risk of death or injury as those in the target area.

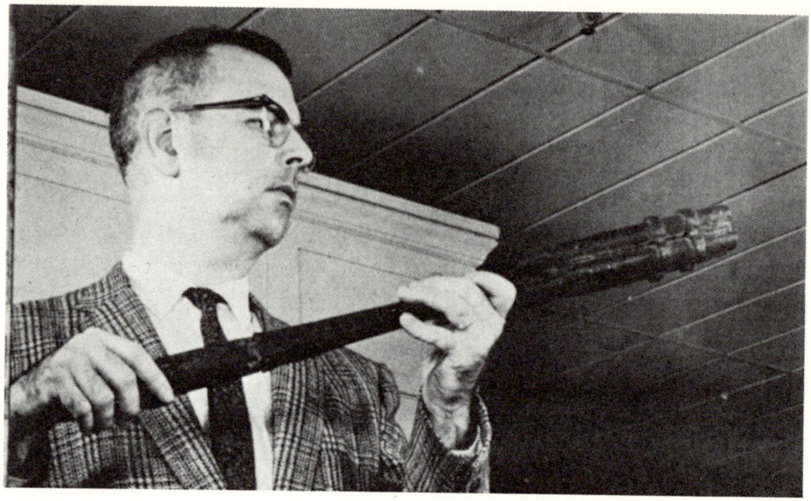

Early handcannon, four-barreled, circa 1450 A.D. Held by Thomas Hall, curator, Winchester Gun Museum, New Haven, Connecticut

Early firearms were clumsy devices, suited only to use as siege weapons, and incapable of being handled by one man. Hand cannons, or "handgonnes" as they were first known, were not far behind, however. Consisting of iron tubes with one end welded shut and with a touch hole drilled at the top near the rear, they were simply small versions of the larger pieces. They were mounted on wooden shafts to facilitate holding during firing.

The Matchlock

In the early part of the 15th Century an improved portable firearm, known as the matchlock, was developed. Here again, the name of the actual inventor is unknown. It is probable that the same basic idea occurred to a number of people at about the same time.

The first matchlock was simply a hand cannon with an "S" shaped iron arm, known as a serpentine, located on a pivot on one side near the breech. A long fuse was fastened to the upper end of this serpentine, by means of a clamp. When the lower end of the serpentine was pulled rearward, the upper portion took the lighted fuse to the touch hole where it ignited the powder. To facilitate ignition, a small depression, known as a flashpan, was made at the mouth of the touchhole. A little powder was poured into this, leading the fire to the main charge.

These first matchlocks were still pretty primitive devices. However, the fuses gave them greater flexibility than earlier firearms. True, ignition still depended on a basic fire source; but once the fuses were lighted, the guns could be carried considerable distances before firing.

Over the years, stocks, resembling those of modern firearms, were developed, enabling the user to fire these pieces from the shoulder. Fuses were improved by soaking them in saltpeter solutions and then drying them, insuring more even burning. Serpentines were improved, to provide more positive action, and hinged covers for flash pans were developed to help keep the powder dry in wet weather.

Improvements in Gunpowder

Gunpowder, too, was improved with the passage of time. Friar Bacon's first product, miraculous though it was, had its limitations. It was a combination of three basic materials (sulphur, saltpeter, and charcoal) ground into a fine powder. Because of its powdery structure, it took on moisture very easily, causing it to form into lumps which burned slowly rather than exploding.

In the mid-16th Century, experimenters found that if they

added a little water to the mixture, when it was being compounded, they could extrude it through sieves to form small pellets. These pellets, when dried, burned far more uniformly and quickly than the fine powder.

The Wheel Lock

The deficiencies of the matchlock cried for an improvement in firearms design. Strangely, a principle known since primitive times—the creation of fire by striking flint against a piece of iron—was the answer. The first application of this idea was the wheel lock, a marvelously complex device not unlike a modern cigarette lighter.

Leonardo da Vinci, the Renaissance master of art and science, made some of the earliest known drawings of wheel locks. His drawings, and later actual production models, show that the device consisted of a steel wheel with a notched rim. The wheel was mounted on a shaft which was connected to a mainspring by means of a short chain. The wheel was wound by a key, wrapping the chain around a shaft and putting tension on the spring. A latch, which was attached to the trigger, held the whole mechanism in position. Pulling the trigger released the latch, permitting the spring to unwind. This made the notched wheel spin rapidly across the piece of flint which was held against the wheel near the flash pan. The resulting sparks ignited the priming powder and the main charge. A latched cover, also connected to the trigger mechanism, kept the priming powder dry until the gun was ready for firing.

Complex though it was, the wheel lock was a great advance. It did away with the necessity of a fire source.

Early Fixed Ammunition

Ammunition improvements accompanied firearms design advances. The first paper cartridges, containers in which a

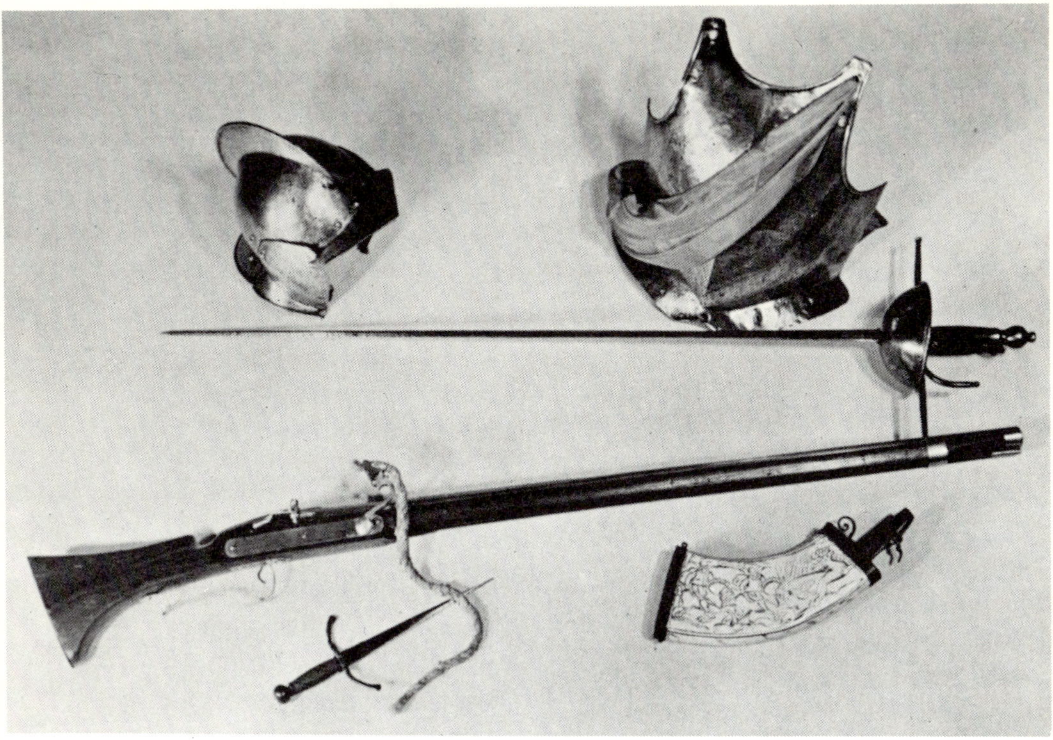

Display of American colonial armament including 17th Century Matchlock

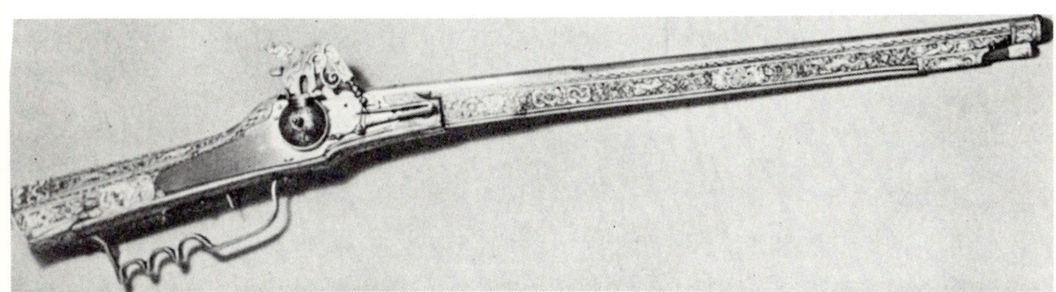

Wheel lock arquebus, circa 1596

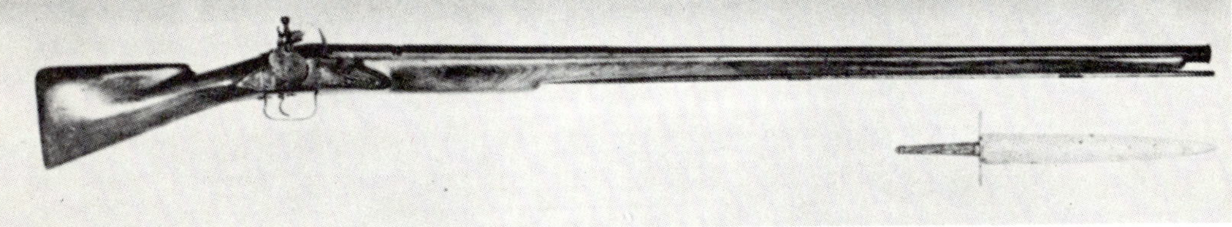

Early English flintlock musket, type known as "doglock," circa 1660

fixed amount of powder was wrapped, were introduced at about the same time as the wheel lock. Sometimes bullets, or charges of shot pellets, were attached to one end of these packages. To load his gun, the shooter tore off one end of the package and poured some of the powder in the priming pan and the rest into the barrel. The bullet or shot charge was then rammed home and the paper was seated on top of the whole charge as a wad to help keep it in place. Though not universally used until much later, these primitive cartridges were employed occasionally as early as the late 15th Century.

The Snapping Lock

The complexity, and consequent high cost, of wheel locks made them the firearms of the well-to-do. Those less well endowed still relied on the matchlock for many more years. Today fine wheel locks, which often incorporated superb workmanship on stocks and metal parts, are prized collector's items and museum pieces.

Firearms designers developed an answer, in time, to the high cost of the wheel lock. The next step, in the evolutionary process, was known as the snapping lock. A sharpened piece of flint was held in a vise-like device on one end of an arm. The other end was fastened to a pin, permitting the arm to move in an arc. A steel bar, also mounted on a pivot, was located opposite the flint-bearing arm with the priming pan below it. A strong spring, actuated by the trigger, forced the flint-bearing arm forward, making the flint strike the steel and sending sparks into the priming pan to ignite the powder charge.

The Flintlock

A French gunsmith, named Marin le Bourgeoys, who lived in the village of Lisieus in the early 17th Century, was responsible for one of the first flintlocks, the next major innovation in firearms design. This new gun combined the best features of all the systems then known. Le Bourgeoys' claim is not undisputed, however. There is some evidence that similar ideas occurred to others about the same time. He documented his work, though, and is thus given major credit.

Le Bourgeoys' new lock system used the interior mechanism of the snapping lock, which had a main spring which bore on a tumbler, and an "L" shaped combination bar and pan cover. He added a new type of sear (the device used to release the spring when the trigger is pulled). This new sear moved vertically instead of laterally, making for stronger actions and permitting the development of truly safe half-cock positions.

The flintlock soon became the standard of the world, remaining in this position until the advent of percussion locks in the early 19th Century. The wars of the 17th and 18th Centuries were fought with these weapons and the fine sporting rifles and shotguns of the day were also flintlocks.

The Origins of Birding

Throughout the period of development of all of these lock systems, "birding" (hunting small game and birds with a shotgun) grew in popularity throughout Europe and this country. In some cases, fowling pieces were a vital necessity as a means of putting food on the table. In others, hunting was purely for sport. One famed form of the fowling piece was the blunderbuss, by legend the popular arm of the pilgrims in this country. While the actual number of such arms used in Colonial America was probably small, there is no doubt that many of these early shotguns were used in Europe. The bell-shaped muzzle was an early attempt (not a very successful one) to achieve a wider dispersion of the shot pattern.

Percussion Firing

The flintlock firearms of the late 18th and early 19th Century were vast improvements over the match and wheel locks of several centuries earlier. However, they still had severe limitations. Powder in the priming pans could still get wet, in spite of all precautions. The guns were slow to load and not always dependable in firing.

Alexander John Forsyth, a Scottish minister with a penchant for inventing things, changed all this. In his studies, he learned about chemical substances called fulminates, which are salts produced by dissolving metals in acids. When struck a hard blow, these salts explode with great force. Substances with these properties include fulminates of gold, silver, and mercury as well as potassium chlorate.

While some earlier experimenters had thought that these substances might be substituted for saltpeter in making gunpowder, Forsyth was the first to recognize their potential as a trouble-free ignition system in themselves. At first he tried substituting fulminates for powder in priming pans. While this sometimes worked, it was far from reliable. After much experimenting, he found that a sharp blow would ignite the fulminates better than sparks. To accomplish this, he designed a lock in which a small quantity of fulminate was ignited by the blow of a cock on a plunger. He built a small rotary magazine which held enough priming mixture for 25 shots and fastened it to the side of the breech on a pivot. When the magazine was given a half turn, a small amount of the substance fell into an ignition chamber. The magazine was then turned back into firing position permitting the plunger to be hit by the cock when the trigger was pulled. The ignition chamber was completely enclosed and designed so that the plunger compressed the fulminate violently when the cock struck it, igniting the substance and sending a flash of flame into the black powder charge in the barrel.

Almost foolproof, Forsyth's design worked nearly every time in all kinds of weather and he received a patent on it in 1807. In spite of its reliability, however, he had little success in selling his invention to military authorities.

The Percussion Cap

An English artist, Joshua Shaw, who emigrated to Philadelphia, is generally credited with devising the best and most enduring percussion system. Known as the percussion cap, it soon became standard the world over. He placed small quantities of fulminate inside little thin gauge copper cylinders shaped somewhat like top hats. The material was held in place with a small piece of metal foil, coated with shellac for waterproofing. These "caps," as they were called, were placed over nipples on the gun's action, which had holes drilled in them leading to the powder charge in the chamber. When the hammer struck the cap, it ignited the fulminate, sending a flash of fire into the powder chamber to set off the charge. Here was a truly portable ignition system, so superior to others then known that there was little comparison.

Progress came fast in the 19th Century. Shaw's system was invented about 1816 and was patented in this country in 1822. By that time several others had devised similar devices. Percussion caps found favor very quickly, particularly for pistols and shotguns where fast firing was a great advantage. While flintlocks were still made, up until the time of the Civil War, the percussion system became standard for sporting firearms long before that time.

The Advent of Breech-Loading

The Civil War, with the tremendous need for military arms it generated, gave particular inspiration to firearms and ammunition designers. It was during this conflict that the idea of breech-loading firearms, firing fixed ammunition, was perfected.

Gun designers had dreamed of this idea for centuries. In fact, a number of experimental breech-loading guns, using paper cartridges, were built long before this time. One such early wheel lock, made in the reign of Henry VIII, is on exhibit in the Tower of London today.

The limiting factor, in the design of breech-loaders, was the problem of containing the gases created by the ignition of the powder. Early designers knew that loading from the breech-end would be far more efficient than loading from the muzzle. The necessary extra opening in the barrel was the stumbling block.

Threaded breech plugs which could be unscrewed for loading were used in cannons as early as the 15th Century. However, the science of metallurgy was not sufficiently developed to permit the extension of this idea to shoulder arms at that time.

The First Center-Fire Shotgun Shell

Even the best designed early breechloaders had a tendency to leak gas to the rear on firing. The first step towards an ultimate solution of this problem was devised by a Frenchman named Samuel Pauly. Although he was fifty years ahead of his time, he devised the first practical self contained cartridge. In many respects, his invention was the forerunner of modern shotgun shells. His gun used the first internal firing pin, a break open breech, an outside cocking lever, and a cartridge in which the primer, for the first time, was located in the center of the head. His cartridge had a brass head and a paper body. Though he had worked out a system not unlike that used in modern firearms and ammunition, his designs were not sufficiently dependable and were never widely used. His concept of a self-contained cartridge, however, set the stage for shotguns as we know them today.

CHAPTER 3

The Development of the Modern Shotgun

It would be misleading to indicate that modern shotguns, and shells for them, were a direct outgrowth of Samuel Pauly's development. There were many intermediate steps in firearms and ammunition design, involving the use of a number of variations of self contained paper or metallic cartridges.

The first fully successful fixed cartridge was not a shotgun shell, but rather a rim fire, very similar to modern .22 caliber rifle cartridges. Horace Smith and Daniel Wesson, remembered today because of the Smith and Wesson handguns that still bear their names, were its developers. In their cartridge, as in modern .22's, the priming mixture was located in a cavity in the rim of the head. Black powder and the bullet were then loaded into the rest of the brass case. Widely used in a number of guns in a variety of calibers, the new rim fire loads were an almost immediate success. The only limitation was one of power Because the metal used in the case had to be sufficiently soft to permit the gun hammer to compress it to set off the priming mixture, heavy powder charges could not be used.

The Perfection of Center-Fire Cartridges

The answer to this problem was the development of center-fire cartridges. In these, the priming mixture, applied in a paste form, is located in a cup inserted in a hole in the center of the brass cartridge head. The gun's firing pin hits the back end of this cup, forcing it against a metal anvil which compresses the compound violently, setting it off to ignite the main powder charge. Location of the primer in the center of the cartridge head permits the use of thicker metal walls and heavier heads, thus eliminating the power limitation problems of the rim fire. Colonel Hiram Berdan, an American Army officer, and Colonel Edward Boxer, a British Army officer, share the honors for developing this idea. The basic designs, developed by both men, are still in use today, though, strangely enough, the Berdan primer, an American development, is used largely in Europe while the Boxer, an English design, is preferred in this country.

Repeating Firearms

The development of rifles, handguns, and shotguns, to use the various new types of fixed cartridges, kept pace with the design of the ammunition itself. The advent of practical rim and center-fire cartridges also made possible the introduction of practical repeating firearms. As was the case with breech loading firearms, the idea of guns capable of firing more than one shot had long intrigued designers. Early efforts in this direction, dating back almost to the beginnings of firearms, usually involved guns with more than one barrel. Some of the first attempts, in the matchlock days, involved as much hazard to the men behind the guns as to those in the target area. Experiments continued, however, and multiple barrel weapons, using every ignition system, from matchlocks to center fire cartridges, have been produced.

In addition to revolving barrels, revolving cylinders were used to make repeating firearms. Modern revolvers still use this idea in which a ratchet system, actuated by the trigger, moves the cylinder after each shot, bringing a new chamber into firing position. Perfection of these weapons came after the invention of the percussion cap. Samuel Colt, the famed designer and manufacturer whose name survives today in Colt handguns, is credited with this perfection, even though the first primitive designs of this type date back to the 16th Century. While some rifles and shotguns using this system were made, they did not work very well. A tight gas seal is almost impossible in revolvers. A gap between the cylinder and the bore, which is inherent in the design, permits the escape of some burning gas on firing. In a revolver, held in one hand, this is no problem; but, in a rifle or a shotgun, where one hand must extend on the fore-end to hold the gun to the shoulder, the hot gas escaping results in burned arms.

The real answer, for effective repeating rifles and shotguns, required the use of a magazine parallel to the axis of the bore and an integral barrel and receiver assembly. While some primitive repeaters of this type were tried in the pre-fixed ammunition days, they were never very satisfactory. With the introduction of rim fire cartridges, however, such designs developed rapidly. The first practical guns of this type were forebears of present day lever action rifles.

The Rise of Sporting Shotguns

The development of shotguns, and ammunition for them, followed the basic patterns of development of other firearms. By the mid 19th Century, the "fowling piece" had achieved a large degree of sophistication. The hunting of upland game and waterfowl, both for sport and food, was very popular and the shotgun was the firearm used.

Since all early firearms had smooth bores, the history of the development of muzzle loading firearms is also the history of the development of shotguns. In the late 18th and early 19th centuries, the introduction of rifled barrels signaled a change. It had long been realized that spiral grooves, cut into the bore of a gun designed to fire a single projectile, could increase its accuracy and range. Improvements in ammunition and firearms designs made this idea practical so that, by the time of the Civil War, smooth bore muskets, except for shotguns, were obsolescent. Although significant numbers of these firearms were used during this conflict, they were hangovers from an earlier time.

The double-barreled, muzzle-loading, percussion lock shotgun, however, was a fixture as a sporting arm for many years, well past the War Between the States. Sportsmen found, soon after the perfection of Joshua Shaw's idea, that this new system was relatively impervious to the effects of weather. In addition, percussion lock guns could be fired and reloaded far more rapidly than flintlocks. Sportsmen, however, were not the only devotees of the system. Percussion lock shotguns were used with great effect by the famed "shotgun riders" of western stage coaches as a defense aaginst marauding bandits.

Center-Fire Shotgun Shells

The advent of breech-loading rifles, however, presaged a similar revolution in shotguns. The necessities of war hastened the change for military weapons; but, once peace was restored, arms designers were free to turn their knowledge to other channels.

Workable center-fire shotgun shells made their appearance in Europe at about the same time as their rifle counterparts. The first such shells had all-brass cases, with center-fire primers. They were generally sold without powder, wads, and shot. Shooters loaded them by hand to their own specifications.

In the early 1870's a far less expensive shell, utilizing a brass head and a body made of tightly wound paper, similar to Pauly's, was developed in England. These were initially sold, primed but unloaded, as their all-brass counterparts had been.

Marcellus Hartley, the founder of the Union Metallic Cartridge Company, saw a market for loaded shotgun shells in this country and his company, a predecessor of what is now Remington Arms Company, Inc., was the first one to produce such ammunition in America. Introduced in the mid 1870's, this new product was not greatly different from modern shotgun shells except that the propellant was black, instead of smokeless, powder.

Choke Boring

Another important step in the progression towards the modern shotgun, was the development of choke boring. Until the post Civil War days, all shotguns had barrels with the same interior dimensions from chamber to muzzle. As a result, their effective range was severely limited. The best of them were only capable of putting about 40 percent of the shot charge in a thirty inch circle at 40 yards.

A man named Fred Kimble, an American professional hunter who shot wild ducks for the market, is generally credited with changing all this. As is so often true in the field of firearms development, his claim as the inventor of choke boring is not undisputed. Regardless of who had the idea first, however, the important thing is that it was found that if the inside diameter of the bore of a shotgun barrel, near the muzzle end, was decreased, this would tend to hold the shot charge together for a longer period of time after it left the muzzle. The idea worked and Kimble and others succeeded in designing barrels which would put up to 70 percent or more of the shot in a thirty inch circle at forty yards. Within a short span of years, all manufacturers were offering choke bored shotguns. Today, a wide variety of degrees of choke are offered, ranging from "cylinder bore" (no choke at all for short range) to "modified" (about "half choke" for medium range), and "full" (for long range).

Smokeless Powder

With the development of breech loading shotguns; center-fire primed, loaded, paper-and-brass shotgun shells; and choke boring, only one further step remained to set the stage for the modern shotgun. This was the development of smokeless powder.

The black powder of Friar Bacon's day, with the few changes noted earlier, was the standard of the world from the 13th Century until the 1880's. Then a French engineer named Paul Vieille, using a variant of the then widely known pyroxylin plastic, famed in baby's celluloid rattles and men's high collars, developed a revolutionary new propellant. Vieille's new smokeless powder used a modification of the pyroxylin formula, combined with ethyl alcohol. At about the same time, Alfred Nobel, the inventor of dynamite, developed a combination of guncotton and nitroglycerin, which was equally effective. Both types of smokeless powder have been in use ever since.

The new powders were soon in great demand. They made it possible to improve the performance of rifles and shotguns by as much as 75 percent. Maximum muzzle velocities, in rifles with black powder, were well under 1500 feet per second. With modern smokeless powders, the top limits are about 4,000 feet per second. This improvement increased range and flattened trajectories for rifle bullets. The new powders were clean burning and, unlike black powder, left little residue in the barrels of rifles and shotguns. Above all, they did not produce the great clouds of smoke, characteristic of black powder.

Smokeless powder, however, created a challenge for metallurgists. Typical internal pressures in a gun barrel were raised from about 20,000 pounds per square inch, to 50,000 pounds or better. Old-fashioned guns just couldn't take this; so new steels and new design concepts had to be worked out.

Smokeless powder spelled the demise of the handsome "damascus" barrel shotguns. These barrels were made by winding red hot strips of steel around a mandrel and then welding them to fuse the metal. The result was a decorative barrel, but the welds were not strong enough to withstand the high pressures of the smokeless powder. Although some shooters, either through lack of information or nostalgia, have persisted in trying to shoot these guns with modern ammunition, with oft times disastrous results, they should be hung on the wall as decorative pieces today, *not* used in the field or over traps. They are just plain dangerous with smokeless powder!

CHAPTER 4

The Shotgun Today

The first modern shotgun, designed to handle center-fire ammunition, utilized the so-called "hinge" or "break open" action. Still popular today, these guns are available in both double and single barreled versions. The doubles are made with barrels located side-by-side, or one-over-the-other, and have a two shot capacity. The singles, obviously, are limited to one shot.

As the names imply, these guns are loaded by breaking the action open on a hinge just behind the breech. High grade doubles are equipped with a device which automatically ejects fired shells when the gun is opened after shooting. The less expensive models have two triggers while the more expensive ones have selective single triggers which give the shooter the option of firing either barrel first.

While single shot, single barrel guns are relatively inexpensive (except for a few "high grade" models used for trap shooting), good quality doubles are very much "carriage trade" models today. Because labor rates are so high in this country and good doubles require a lot of hand work, there are very few such guns now made in the United States. A number of imports are available, at medium to high prices, and there are one or two low-priced doubles still made here. As far as domestically produced shotguns are concerned, however, other action styles predominate.

Bolt Action

While bolt action rifles are very popular the world over, their use, in shotguns, is limited to some very inexpensive models. The principle of their design is based on the idea of using a bolt, similar to that used to fasten a door, to lock a shell in the breech of a gun. Originally conceived in Germany in the 1820's, this idea was perfected, after the advent of fixed ammunition, by a noted German designer, Peter Paul Mauser. The Mauser action, still in use today, was the forebear of all modern bolt action designs.

The limitation of this action style in shotguns is its relatively slow speed of operation. While this is no problem in a high-powered, big-game rifle, where game is taken at relatively long ranges (and is apt to be relatively still when shot), it presents real difficulties when trying to get off two or more rapid shots at a fast flushing game bird.

Pump or Slide Action

The pump or slide action is one of the most popular styles of American made shotguns. The fastest of hand-operated guns, it uses a movable fore-end to work the action. The fore-end, usually made of wood, is attached to a bar or pair of bars which in turn are fastened to the bolt. When the fore-end is moved to the rear, it pushes back the bar or bars, opening the bolt. As the bolt opens, it forces the hammer downward cocking the gun and ejecting the empty shell. A spring in the tubular magazine, located beneath the barrel and between the action bars, and a carrier device then lift a new shell into position. When the fore-end is moved forward to close the action, the bolt pushes the shell into the chamber and the gun is again ready for firing.

Pump action shotguns can be single-loaded through the action port if desired, or they can hold up to five shells, one in the chamber and four in the magazine. For waterfowl hunting, where Federal law limits guns to a three shot capacity, a plug is placed in the magazine so that it will only hold two shells.

Semi-Automatic or Autoloading Action

The semi-automatic or autoloading action is also extremely popular. Essentially these shotguns are ones that can be fired repeatedly just by pulling the trigger. The action operates automatically as each shot is fired, ejecting the expended shell and moving a new one into firing position. Although these guns are often called automatics, they do not qualify for this definition. A true automatic is a machine gun which keeps firing as long as the shooter keeps the trigger depressed. Such guns are illegal for hunting use and for this reason, in the semi-automatic or autoloader, the trigger must be pulled for each shot.

There are two basic types of autoloaders. The first uses the force of recoil while the second utilizes the power created by the burning gases of ignited gunpowder.

The simplest recoil operated actions are those of the so-called "blow back" type. In these, the breech block is held in the locked position by a spring. When the gun is fired, the projectile is propelled out of the barrel by the force of expanding gases. The recoil effect, created by this, pushes the bolt back into the open position, ejecting the empty cartridge. The tension on the spring then forces the bolt forward into the closed position, picking up another cartridge from the magazine on the way and putting it into the chamber. While this system is suitable for use with relatively low powered firearms, such as handguns and rim fire .22 caliber rifles, it is not strong enough for use with high powered rifles or shot guns.

Retarded blow backs, a variation of this system, use either a toggle or screw-threaded locking lugs on the front of the bolt to lock it more firmly in position. This allows the use of more powerful ammunition.

Either a short or a long recoil system is used with retarded blow back actions. In short systems, the bolt and barrel are locked together as described above. When the gun is fired, both move to the rear for a short distance. By the time the shot charge has left the muzzle, the rearward motion of the barrel has stopped. The breech block unlocks and the momentum started by the expansion of the burning gases of the powder charge drives the bolt further to the rear, permitting the ejection of the fired shell. A spring then moves the block forward, while another shell is picked up from the magazine. As the action locks up again, the new shell is fed into the chamber and the gun is again ready to fire. Widely used in semi-automatic pistols, this system has also been adapted to some shotguns.

The long recoil system differs in that the barrel and block stay together during the entire recoil cycle instead of separating after a short rearward travel. When the block has gone as far back as it can go, it unlocks from the barrel and is momentarily held back while the barrel is carried forward by a spring. When the barrel reaches its normal position, it hits a latch which releases the bolt. A spring then takes the bolt forward, a new shell is fed up from the magazine, and the gun locks up, ready for firing again. John Browning, one of America's gun designing geniuses, invented this system and it is still used on a number of modern shotguns including models made by both Remington and Browning.

An entirely different principle is involved in gas operated autoloaders. In these, a small hole is drilled in the bottom of the barrel slightly forward of the chamber. When the gun is fired, some of the gas, created by the ignition of the powder charge, is vented through this hole. There it actuates a piston-like device, located in the fore-arm. Action bars, or a rod, are attached to this device and to the bolt. As the piston is driven to the rear by the gases, it unlocks the bolt forcing it backward. In a cycle of operation similar to that of recoil operated systems, the fired shell is ejected, a spring moves the bolt forward again, a new shell is picked up from the magazine, and the gun locks up ready for firing again. This system, or variations of it, is used in a number of modern military weapons as well as in several sporting shotguns and rifles. In fact, gas operated autoloaders are fast coming to the fore as one of the most popular action styles today.

Lever Actions

While very few lever action shotguns have been manufactured, no discussion of this subject would be complete without a mention of this type. Used primarily in hunting rifles, it traces its lineage back to the Civil War. Basically, it has a hinged lever, which also forms the guard for the trigger, located at the bottom of the receiver. The bolt, locking mechanism, and the device used to lift cartridges from the magazine to the chamber, are actuated by moving the lever up and down. Since the whole system is capable of firing almost as quickly as the pump action, it's hard to say why it hasn't found wider use in shotguns.

Shotgun Gauges

The measurement of the size of shells used in shotguns is known as "gauge," as opposed to the term "caliber" which is used to describe the sizes of rifle bullets. Ancient in origin, it tells how many round balls, of equal size, may be obtained from a pound of lead. If twelve such balls constitute a pound, a gun designed to fire one of them, as a solid projectile, was known as a 12 gauge. If sixteen could be obtained, the gun designed to fire one was a 16 gauge. The designations go on through 10, 20 and 28 gauges. The smallest of modern shotguns, the .410, is not actually a gauge but, rather, a caliber. Thus a .410 gun has a bore with an inside diameter of .410 inches. Round lead balls are no longer fired in shotguns. However the measurement system still prevails.

The question of what gauge should be used for various types of shooting is largely a matter of personal choice. 12, 16, and 20 gauges are the most popular—in order of mention. However, 20 gauge guns are fast rising in favor. As a rule of thumb, remember that larger gauges offer more shot pellets in the shell. It is also important to remember that smaller gauge guns are usually lighter and more easy to handle. Because their ammunition contains less powder and shot, their recoil is also lighter. The best guide line, however, is that larger gauges are best suited for larger birds and animals and vice versa.

28 and .410 gauge guns, though sometimes used for hunting, are in a special category. Their main use is confined to small upland game and skeet shooting.

Choke Boring

We have already discussed the origins of choke boring. A vital consideration in the choice of a gun, choke is a partial constriction of the bore at the muzzle end. Its purpose is to control the shot pattern. Different degrees of choke boring make it possible to alter the spread of the shot charge to provide the optimum distribution at various distances. It is axiomatic that the tighter the choke, the longer the effective range of the shotgun.

To demonstrate this point, the inside diameter of the bore of a 12 gauge shotgun is .730 inches. In a full choke 12 gauge, the diameter at the muzzle end of the barrel is tapered to .694 inches. This constriction of .036 inches is sufficient to tighten the shot pattern to the point where 70 percent of the shot will go in a 30 inch circle at 40 yards. As we have seen, this is known as full choke boring and it is best suited for long range use.

Actually choke affects shot patterns in much the same fashion as the nozzle of a garden hose affects a stream of water. The tighter the nozzle is turned, the narrower the stream becomes and the further it carries. Opening the nozzle widens the stream and decreases the effective range.

Regardless of gauge, the various degrees of choke boring offered today are designed to put the approximate percentages of shot listed below in a 30 inch circle at 40 yards:

Choke	Percentage of shot in 30 inch circle at 40 yards
Full	70
Modified	60
Improved Cylinder	50
Cylinder or Skeet	40

From this it can readily be seen that a shooter should select chokes on the basis of the approximate range at which most of his shooting will be done.

The "pass shooting" waterfowler, whose targets are usually 40 or more yards away, wants a full choke 12 gauge. The upland hunter who is after pheasants or partridge at ranges of less than 30 yards, can best use a modified or improved cylinder gun of either 12, 16, or 20 gauge. The quail or woodcock hunter, whose quarry is limited to small birds at short ranges, wants an improved cylinder gun of 20 gauge or less.

Barrel Lengths

Modern shotguns are offered with barrels of 26, 28, 30 or, occasionally 32, inches in length. There used to be a theory that longer barrels imparted greater velocities to the shot charge. Ballistics experts, however, agree that this is not true. Actually, the shot charge reaches its maximum speed in about the first 20 inches of the barrel. After that, length has little effect on velocity. The only valid reason for long barrels is that their greater length provides a longer sighting radius for more accurate pointing at extreme ranges. Shorter barrels are usually preferred for close range hunting and shooting because they handle more easily for quick shots.

Stock Dimensions

There was a day when stock dimensions of a shotgun were usually fitted to the individual specifications of the buyer. Gun stores had so called "try guns," with adjustable parts. The customer was fitted for a stock in much the same manner that he might be fitted for a custom made suit. Today, this is a luxury which the average shooter can hardly afford to indulge. True, Abercrombie and Fitch and similar stores are still equipped to perform this service and they occasionally are called upon to do so—for an expensive custom made gun—however, the average shooter buys "ready-made" stocks. Minor adjustments, such as the addition, or reduction, of an inch in length, or a slight change in drop or pitch, can be had on special order from factories at additional cost.

Over the years, gun manufacturers have developed some pretty comprehensive statistics on the most popular stock sizes. As a result, they have developed standard stock dimensions that are pretty well suited to most people. Thus the average man can usually pick a gun off the rack in a store and it will fit him fairly well. If he has an unusually long neck, particularly short or long arms, or some other physical aberration, he may need minor or major alterations but this is the exception rather than the rule.

The only major differences in stock shapes are the variations between field (or skeet) and trap dimensions. Because trap targets are shot going away without too much rise, shooters find that stocks with a straighter comb are better than those with more drop.

Muzzle Devices

Most modern pump and autoloading shotguns are so designed that barrels can be interchanged, within gauges, without any special fitting or tools. Thus a shooter with a 12 gauge pump gun with a full choke barrel can buy an extra modified or improved cylinder barrel (or both) and, in effect, have one gun he can use for three different types of shooting. Even though the regular barrel can be removed and the alternate put in its place in a matter of seconds, is it hardly convenient for a shooter to carry extra barrels with him in the field. As a partial answer to this problem, a number of variable choke devices have been devised. Essentially these are gadgets that are permanently attached to the muzzle of the gun. In some, the change from full to open choke can be made by turning the device much as the nozzle of a hose is turned to adjust the spray. In others, short tubes of various dimensions are inserted in the choke controller in a matter of seconds. While not quite as effective as different barrels designed for different uses, these muzzle devices do make one gun with one barrel more versatile.

CHAPTER 5

Modern Ammunition

The experienced scattergun enthusiast seldom has much trouble deciding what shotgun shell he should use for various types of shooting. He has learned the answers through years of experience. For the novice, however, the wide variety of gauges, shot sizes and loads offered can be confusing at best.

Unquestionably, there is a great deal of overlapping. However, there are guide lines which can help the neophyte. Let's take a look at the basic construction of shotgun shells, the types of shells available, and the types of game for which each is best suited.

Shotgun Shell Construction

As we know from Chapter 3, the modern shotgun shell evolved, in something like its present form, in the early 1870's. Essentially, this early shell consisted of a tube of tightly wound paper set in a brass head. The interior of the head was reinforced with a base wad of treated cardboard. A center-fire primer was located in the rear of the brass exterior. Powder was loaded on top of the base wad and overpowder and filler wads (of varying sizes according to the strength of the charge) were placed over the powder. Shot of varying sizes was then put in the tube followed by a cardboard top wad to keep the whole business in place. A lip of the cardboard tube was then rolled down over the top wad (to hold it in place) and the whole shell was complete. Numerous variations in shot size, powder loadings and wadding made it possible to produce shells, from the same basic components, for almost every type of shooting.

Changes in this basic design occurred rapidly over the years. Obviously smokeless powder, after its introduction, replaced black powder as the propellant force. In the 1920's Remington Arms Company introduced non-corrosive priming mixtures. Quickly copied by other shell manufacturers, this new development made it unnecessary to clean guns after each firing. Modern ballistics research resulted in changes in wad structure and shot specifications.

By the late '30's and early '40's a new type of crimp appeared which soon replaced the roll crimp-top wad construction. The old cardboard top wads had an unhappy way of occasionally getting mixed up with the shot pattern, after it left the muzzle, ruining its effectiveness. The so-called "flat top" crimp, in which part of the shell body is folded over the shot charge in a pleated, pie-cut fashion, changed this. The new crimps open up on firing releasing the shot charge to fly, uninhibited, to the target.

Plastic Shells

In 1960, Remington Arms introduced plastic-bodied shells. These new loads, unlike paper, are impervious to the effects of weather. They are scuff and mar proof and will not swell when exposed to moisture, as will paper shells. More important, they maintain ballistic stability far better than paper shells since they seal out the effects of temperature changes on powder. They are far easier to feed into guns, particularly autoloaders. The obvious advantages of plastics, as shell body materials, were so apparent that most other manufacturers have since followed Remington's lead and now offer similar loads.

Shot Containers

Another basic problem, with old fashioned shot shells, was the abrasive effect of the barrel on shot pellets during firing. Pellets on the outside of the pattern tended to rub against the interior of the barrel walls, flattening them so that they wouldn't fly truly. This tended to affect the pattern because these flattened pellets went wide of the mark. Shotshell designers had long recognized this problem and patents were filed, as far back as the 1880's, on materials in which the shot could be wrapped to protect it on its way down the bore. None of these early ideas worked very well, however. Several years ago, the Winchester-Western Division of Olin Mathieson, came up with the idea of wrapping the shot charge in a strip of thin plastic. This did the trick by protecting the shot from abrasion in the bore and then falling away from the pattern after the charge left the muzzle. Improvements came fast with the introduction, by Remington-Peters, of a self-contained plastic wad and shot protector. Now almost all manufacturers offer similar devices which result in greatly improved patterns.

Basic Shotgun Shell Types

The three basic types of shells offered today are: field or low base, long range or high base, and magnum. Each general class contains a variety of load and shot size combinations as well as gauges.

While the designations of low base and high base have less relevance, in this day of plastic-bodied shells, than they had in the days of paper, they provide an easy means for differentiating between field and long range loads because the terms mean just what they say. On field loads the metal base does not extend as high up on the plastic or paper tube as it does

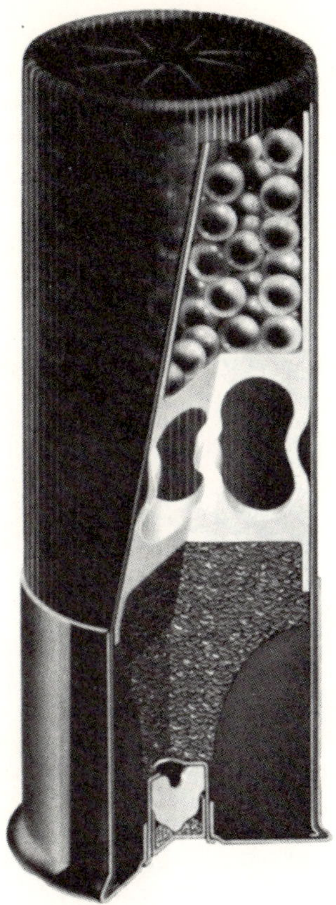

Cross section of modern high-base plastic shotshell

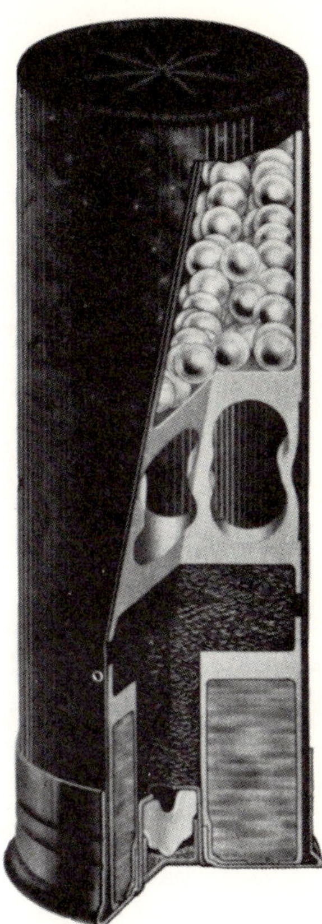

Cross section of modern low-base plastic shotshell

on long range loads. Historically the reason for this is that field loads create lower internal pressures on ignition than do long range loads. Hence they do not need as much metal to contain these pressures. The replacement of paper bodies with plastic and the use of new, stronger base wad materials has changed this to some extent. However, high base loads are still made with more metal in the head than low base.

Low Base Shells

Low base (or field load) shotgun shells are available in 12, 16 and 20 gauges. Basically, these loads are designed for use on small upland game birds and animals at relatively short ranges. They cost less than high base shells and are entirely adequate, in most situations, for game such as rabbits, grouse, partridge, quail, doves, and woodcock. Target loads, intended for trap and skeet shooting, are also of the low base type, except for 28 and .410 gauge target shells which are high base.

High Base Shells

High base loads, which are available in 10, 12, 16, 20, 28 and .410 gauges, are intended for use in hunting larger birds and animals such as geese, ducks, pheasants, turkey and fox. They are also used for game such rabbits, squirrels and larger western grouse when shooting is done at longer ranges.

In 12, 16, 20 and 28 gauges, the standard length of both low and high base shells is 2¾ inches. In 10 gauge, standard shells are offered in 2¾ and 2⅞ inch lengths. In .410 gauge, shells are available in 2½ and 3 inch lengths. Most .410 gauge guns are chambered to handle 3 inch shells and those of 2½ inch size will also work in them.

Magnum Shells

Magnum loads are offered in both 2¾ and 3 inch long sizes. The standard chamber length for most modern guns is 2¾ inches and it is not safe to fire 3 inch shells in guns other than those with 3 inch chambers. Most firearms manufacturers, however, produce special magnum models designed for use with the longer shells.

The purpose of magnum shells, whether they are $2\frac{3}{4}$ or 3 inches in length, is to provide extra knockdown power and range. They are loaded with more powder and shot than standard shells and are designed for use on larger birds, such as geese and turkeys, at extreme ranges.

Special Shells

Other additions, to standard high base loadings, are rifled slug and buckshot shells. A rifled slug is a solid, cylindrical lead projectile with rifling grooves cut into its side. In theory, these grooves impart a spin to the slug when it is fired from a smooth bore gun. Buckshot shells are loaded with a number of large lead pellets, far bigger than the largest of standard shot sizes. Both rifled slugs and buckshot are designed for use on larger animals such as deer, black bear and wolf. Because they are relatively short range weapons, firing heavy projectiles, they are often preferred for big game hunting in relatively populated areas where high powered rifles would not be safe to use.

So called scatter or spreader loads are also offered in low base shells. Designed to spread the shot pattern over a wide area, they are usually used to give an open pattern for fast flushing game when a full or modified choke barrel is being used.

Shot Sizes

Each of the main classes of shotgun shells, described above, is offered with a variety of shot sizes. While no hard and fast rules on shot sizes can be set forth, because so many variables enter the picture (such as type and extent of cover, size of game, etc.), it is generally safe to go on the principle that the smaller the game, the smaller the size of shot you should use. In describing shot sizes, the low numbers (2, 4, and 5) indicate larger shot while the high numbers (6, 7, 8 and 9) indicate smaller sizes. The following table offers a good guide line for the novice on what sizes to use for various types of shooting:

TYPE OF GAME	SHOT SIZES (ALL GAUGES)
Ducks	4, 5, 6
Geese	BB, 2, 4
Pheasants	5, 6
Grouse and Partridge	5, 6, 7½, 8
Quail	7½, 8, 9
Doves and Pigeons	6, 7½, 8
Woodcock	7½, 8, 9
Rabbits	4, 5, 6
Squirrels	5, 6
Rail	7½, 8, 9
Turkey	BB, 2, 4
Fox	BB, 2
Deer, Black Bear, Wolf	Rifled slug or Buckshot
Crows	6, 7½
Skeet and trap shooting	7½, 8, 9

Shot Production

Among the outstanding landmarks of a number of cities, ranging from Bridgeport and New Haven, Connecticut, to East Alton, Illinois, and Anoka, Minnesota, are their shot towers. The principle behind these structures dates back to colonial days. Among the many interesting characteristics of molten lead is the fact that, when passed through a sieve-like device and dropped from a height, it breaks into a spray of drops. Unlike water drops which, when released from comparable heights, take on a tear shaped configuration, lead drops form into near perfect spheres.

This is the fundamental principle of the shot towers. At the base of these towers, metal pigs made of alloys of lead and various hardening agents such as antimony, are loaded

SHOT	APPROX. PELLETS IN 1 OZ.	2385	585	410	350	225	170	135	90	50
	DIAM. IN INCHES	.05	.08	.09	.09½	.11	.12	.13	.15	.18
	NUMBER	12	9	8	7½	6	5	4	2	BB

BUCKSHOT	APPROX. PELLETS IN 1 LB.	340	300	175	145	130
	DIAM. IN INCHES	.24	.25	.30	.32	.33
	NUMBER	4	3	1	0	00

Comparative sizes of shot and buckshot

Comparative bore sizes (half of actual size, l. to r.): 10 gauge (.775″), 12 gauge (.730″), 16 gauge (.670″), 20 gauge (.615″), 28 gauge (.550″) and .410 bore (.410″).

into elevators which take them to the top. There, the pigs are melted and poured into sieve-like frying pans. The size of the holes in the bottom of these pans determines the size of the shot to be made. The molden, lead-drops fall some 190 feet from the pans, into a bath of water. The droplets take on their spherical shape almost immediately after leaving the pan and the water serves only to cushion their fall.

The resulting pellets are collected from the water bath,

dried, and again transported almost to the top of the tower where they are run through tumblers to polish them. The shot then travels down a series of inclined planes. Absolutely round shot negotiates this obstacle course with ease but pellets that are out of round fall into troughs and are taken back for remelting. At the end of this process, the product is graded for size and fed into storage bins preparatory for loading into shells or sale as a component for hand loaded ammunition.

Although many attempts have been made to improve on this method of making shot, no others, so far, have been as successful. This simple, centuries-old process is as efficient as many modern, fully automated manufacturing techniques used for other products. Indeed the classic shot tower was one of the first truly automated production techniques ever developed.

Dram Equivalent

Among the more confusing descriptions used, in connection with ammunition, is the term "dram equivalent." In the days of black powder shotguns, the power of a load was described in terms of the amount of powder used rather than by an attempt to analyze the speed with which the shot charge would travel. Ballistics, in those days, was a rather inexact science at best and velocities varied quite a bit. As a result loads were designated by the weight of the powder charge. The avoirdupois dram, which is 1/16 of an ounce, was a convenient unit of measure to use, and loads were defined by the number of drams of black powder they contained—3 drams, 4 drams, etc.

No one could carry scales with them in the hunting field, so scoops of the correct size to contain a given weight of powder were developed. Even today, with modern production techniques, powder charges are often measured by volume rather than weight.

Early smokeless powders were made to load on the basis of

equal bulk with black powder. The idea was that a shell loaded with 3 drams of smokeless powder would have ballistics comparable to one loaded with three drams of black powder.

Progress in smokeless powder development changed all this, and soon these newer propellants no longer even came close to a bulk-for-bulk performance with black powder. The old terminology for describing the strength of loads has persisted, however, Shooters knew what sort of performance they could expect from 3 drams of black powder and so ammunition manufacturers continued to designate smokeless powder loads, designed for similar results, as "3 drams equivalent," even though they might use only a fraction of this weight of smokeless powder. It would be highly dangerous indeed for a reloader to try to use dram equivalent figures as a guide for powder charges. However, the term is a convenience as long as its limitations are recognized.

CHAPTER 6

How to Hit Flying Targets

There's no other excitement quite like it! Whether it's a covey of quail surging up from close cover, a clay target thrown on a trap or skeet field, a pintail duck winging in low over decoys, or only a tin can tossed high in the air by a companion; hitting flying targets with a shotgun has a thrill all its own!

For the tyro, the question is: how to master the skill. Thousands of words have been written on the subject, but, as with any other sport, it's pretty difficult to become an expert by just reading. In the last analysis, practice is the only answer.

There are, however, some basic fundamentals that can be set down which can start the beginner off on the right foot; saving him from lots of mistakes which would crop up if he tried to learn by the trial and error method.

The most important thing to remember about shooting a shotgun at a flying object of any kind is that the target is moving. If that sounds somewhat obvious, any experienced scattergunner can tell you that most flying targets are missed because people shoot behind them. Stated more simply, they shoot with the barrel pointed at the spot where the target *is* at the time the trigger is touched off, rather than having it pointed at the spot where the target is going to *be* when the shot charge reaches it.

Perhaps the best way to visualize the problem is to remember that a shotgun, in effect, throws out a string of lead shot much as a hose throws out a stream of water. Suppose, for the sake of discussion, that you are standing in your back

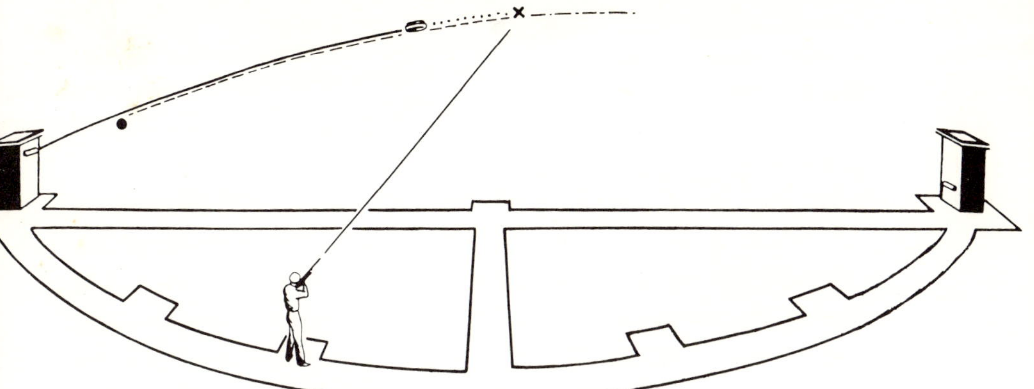

Example of "lead" on a skeet field

yard with the hose turned on. If you want to try to hit a dog running across your lawn with the stream of water, you have to spray it ahead of him so that he will run into it. Another analogy is to consider the problem of a football player throwing a pass to an end running down the field. If the pass receiver is going to catch the ball, the passer has to toss it to a point where the receiver is going to be, not where he is at the moment of throwing.

There are three basic means of putting the shot charge where the target is going to be, rather than where it is at the moment of shooting. The first is called "spot shooting," the second is "pointing out" and the third (and most effective) is the "swing and follow through" system. Let's look at each in turn.

Spot Shooting

In effect, a spot shooter estimates where the target is going to be when he pulls the trigger and points the gun there. He shoots fast and hopes he has figured the problem correctly. There are a few fairly good shots who use this system but they are the exception rather than the rule. Actually, the spot shooter is somewhat akin to the legendary "quick draw" artists of the old West. The stories of their prowess with guns were more legendary than factual. While it is true that an occasional spot shot is necessary, to hit a fast flushing upland bird before it disappears in the brush, for example, the beginning shooter should avoid this technique like the plague. At best, spot shooting is very difficult and it is hardly the way to master the sport.

Pointing Out

The so-called "pointing out" method is a step in the right direction. In this technique, the shooter tries to compute a conscious amount of lead, or how far ahead of the target he should shoot, but he combines this with a swing and follow through. Many books and articles on trap and skeet shooting have been written in which the authors try to tell the shooter how far he should lead a bird flying at a given station. For example, it may be suggested that a shooter should lead the high house bird at station five, on a skeet field, by six feet (or some other distance depending on who is doing the suggesting). There are shooters who claim they can raise a gun to their shoulder, swing it along the path of flight of the target until they are a given distance ahead of it, pull the trigger, hit the bird, and continue the swing in a follow through motion. If your mind works like an IBM machine and you can program it to solve a complex problem in spherical trigonometry and coordinate your body with it, this is the system for you. For most people, however, it's too complicated.

Remember that a flying target, be it animate or inanimate, is moving in a three dimensional plane at speeds up to 70 miles an hour. It may be crossing and rising or crossing and falling all at the same time. If it's a live critter, it may change

Pointing out shooting

from a quartering, going away, dropping target to a rising, straight away with a flip of its tail feathers. Even a clay target may change direction at the whim of a puff of breeze.

Swing and Follow Through

For these reasons, many top flight shooters have found that the "swing and follow through" system works best. In this method, the shooter raises his gun to his shoulder the moment he sees the target. He swings the gun along the path of flight catching up with the target and passing it. The moment the muzzle passes the target, he pulls the trigger *and continues to swing his gun in a follow through motion.* By swinging the gun through the target, he actually computes the rate at which it is moving automatically. He must swing faster for a quartering, right or left angle, target than for a straight away shot. This varying rate of swing, if it is continued after the trigger is pulled, helps to keep the muzzle pointed sufficiently ahead of the target to insure consistent hits.

Obviously, there are other problems, too. Most people who miss rising birds, do so because they shoot under them. Another common mistake is failure to keep the head down on the stock. Just as a golfer tops the ball (or misses it completely) by looking up before he hits it, so many a shooter fails to connect by pulling his head up before he shoots. The result is that while his eyes follow the flight path of the target, the gun barrel doesn't, and he misses.

The primary reason for missed targets, however, is stopping the gun swing at the instant of pulling the trigger. Whether the shooter realizes it or not, there is a built in lag between the instant the brain says "pull the trigger" and the time the message gets to the finger. This lag, maybe only a fraction of a second, is sufficient to let the target get away—unless the

Swing and follow through shooting

shooter continues his swing and follow through in one easy, flowing motion.

Emphasis has been put on the swing and follow through idea as the most important point in hitting flying targets, because without this concept, the battle is lost before it begins. However, there are a number of other fundamentals which are also important.

Good Shooting Form

Because many shooters are more or less self taught, large numbers of them violate some of the basic rules of good form —and get away with it. In numerous cases, these people are pretty effective shots. In spite of their bad form, they manage to fill their game bags and to break a fair percentage of clay targets. The reason, of course, is that they have learned to "groove" their swings and even though they are not doing it right, they achieve consistency. However, if they had learned the fundamentals properly at the start, or would take the trouble to go back and learn them now, they could easily become much better shots.

Of course, the same thing is true of many other sports. All of us have seen golfers, tennis players or even tiddley-winkers whose form is abysmal but who play creditable games. However, the really top-flight performers in any sport usually share some basic fundamentals. Let's look at the fundamentals of good shotgun shooting form to see what they are.

Proper Stance

The key to good stance is to be in a relaxed position which will permit you to swing the gun in whatever direction the target may fly. To achieve this the knees should be bent, ever so slightly, and you should be able to lean slightly in the direction in which you are going to shoot. If you don't do this and stand stiff legged with your weight on your heels, your ability to swing freely will be cramped and the gun's recoil will throw you off balance so that you will have little chance of getting off a successful second shot.

Your feet should be fairly close together so that you can change your weight from one to the other and pivot your body as you swing the gun. About a foot apart is best, though this may vary according to the size of the individual. A right handed person should try to shoot with the left foot advanced while the lefty should reverse the procedure. The upper portion of your body should be held at an angle with the shooting shoulder about 45 degrees from the direction in which the swing will start when the gun is mounted.

Of course, it's simple enough to assume the proper stance when shooting clay targets where you can get all set and then call for the bird. It's a different matter, however, when you are approaching a setter on point and don't know which way the bird will flush. Obviously in field shooting, you can't be sure you'll be standing in just the perfect position when the bird appears. However, if you practice proper stance on clay target fields or with a hand trap, you will find it begins to come almost instinctively in the field. And obviously it will help you break more targets in the inanimate shooting games.

Proper Gun Mounting

Perhaps the key thing to remember, in bringing a shotgun up to your shoulder to shoot, is that the gun stock should come up to your face. Many a tyro makes the mistake of putting the gun up to his shoulder and then bringing his head down so that his face is against the stock. There are two things wrong with this procedure. First of all, in bringing your face down to the stock you usually tilt your head. This means your eyes are on an angle, in relation to the top of the barrel, making it almost impossible to see the target properly. Secondly, you may not get your face all the way down with the result that you see too much of the barrel. This has the same effect as picking your head off the stock; you miss the target by shooting over it. The analogy of the golfer looking up before he hits the ball applies here again.

In bringing the gun up to your shoulder and face, you should thrust it out away from your body and then bring the butt back solidly into position. If you bring the gun up in a direct motion, it's easy to snag it in your clothing or even catch the stock under your arm. This will destroy your timing and probably make you miss.

One or Two Eyes

For some reason, lost in antiquity, in aiming a gun of any kind, many people tend to shut or squint one eye. However, most shotgun experts condemn this procedure except for people who have a left master eye and are right handed or vice versa. The reason is that closing one eye, or squinting it, narrows the field of vision and destroys the ability to judge distance. Nature provided us with two eyes to enable us to perceive depth and to estimate the distance between objects some distance away. It, therefore, seems silly to handicap this ability in shooting by shutting or squinting one eye.

Point, Don't Aim

The correct procedure is to mount the gun to the shoulder with both eyes open focused on the target, not the barrel. Unlike a rifle, a shotgun is pointed not aimed. You should remember that you have a large shot pattern to work with. Seventy percent of the shot will go within a 30 inch circle at

Proper gun mounting

Improper gun mounting

40 yards with a full-choke gun, and your job is to put that shot where the moving target is. Thus, you should only see the barrel in relation to that moving target. To go back to our analogy of a hose, a stream of water and a dog running across the lawn, when you point the hose, you look at the dog, not the nozzle, if you want to hit the animal.

This is the exact opposite of the rifle or pistol shooter who lines up the front and rear sight with the target to achieve hits on a relatively stationary object. This shooter can afford to

Head lifted off stock

Head properly positioned on stock

take the time to line up the sights with precision. In fact, he has to if he expects to hit the target with his one projectile. If a shotgunner were to do this, however, the fast flying target would be long gone before he ever got set.

The Master Eye

Everyone has one eye which is the controlling one. In most cases this master eye follows the master hand, i.e., a right handed shooter has a right master eye. However, there are people who are right handed, yet have a left master eye or vice versa. If this is the case, these people will have trouble shooting with both eyes open unless they can learn to shoot from the shoulder which corresponds with their master eye.

To find out why this is true, and to find out which is your master eye, try this simple test. Keep both eyes open and point your finger at an object some distance away from you. Then shut your left eye (if you are right handed). Your eye and finger will still be lined up with the object if your right eye is the master one. Now open your left eye and shut the right one. In this case, if your right eye is the master one, your finger will appear to jump to the right in relation to the object. If, however, your finger appeared to move in relation to the object when you shut your left eye and stayed lined up when you closed the right one, your left eye is the master one. The converse would be true for left handed people.

As you can see from this test, shooting with both eyes open, for a person whose master eye is the opposite from his master hand, presents problems. The master eye tends to dominate in the process of pointing a gun just as it does in pointing your finger. If this eye is not on the same side as your master hand, you had better forget what we said about keeping both eyes open. Go ahead and squint or shut one eye if you want—or else learn to shoot from the opposite shoulder.

There are a number of people with left master eyes who

are right handed and shoot from the right shoulder successfully. While they are handicapped in depth perception and range estimation, experience can help them to overcome these problems.

Patterning Shotguns

Although modern shotguns are made to exacting standards, there are, inevitably, minor differences in shooting characteristics of different guns—even when they are the same model and gauge. For this reason, it's a good idea when you acquire a new gun to find out where it shoots. This is a relatively simple process, known as patterning. Tack up a large sheet of paper against a safe backstop. Put a black mark in the middle of the paper and inscribe a 30 inch circle around it. Step back to 40 yards, aim at the mark and fire. Try this with several sheets of paper. By checking the dispersion of shot around the mark, you will be able to tell whether your gun is shooting dead center, high, low, to the right or to the left. You can then adjust your handling of the gun accordingly. Of course if the average pattern is consistently way off, you may want to have a gunsmith check your gun for you.

In summary, then, the basic rules for the beginning scattergunner are: swing and follow through, learn the correct stance, bring the gun to the face—not the face to the gun—and point rather than aim. To these add one more item: shoot quickly and smoothly. Put the whole group together and practice, practice, practice. If you do, practicing enough to make the rules a part of your habit pattern, you'll get the full measure of fun and excitement out of gunning for flying targets with a shotgun, and you'll come home with a full bag or a high score at the traps.

CHAPTER 7

Clay Target Shooting

According to *Webster's Collegiate Dictionary,* a clay pigeon is defined as "a saucer of baked clay or other material to be thrown, with a scaling motion, from a trap, for a target in trap (or skeet) shooting." The good worthies who compiled this tome further define a trap as: "a machine for throwing into the air balls, clay pigeons, etc., to be shot *at*." Both definitions are accurate, as far as they go, excluding the perhaps archaic notion that a preposition is a poor word with which to end a sentence.

To the inveterate clay pigeon fan, however, these descriptions hardly scratch the surface. In the first place, clay pigeon (or clay target) shooting involves a great deal more than is implied in the words chosen by this and other dictionaries. In the second place, the two most popular clay pigeon (or clay target) games, trap shooting and skeet shooting, require considerable skill which, in the interests of brevity, has been overlooked by the lexicographers.

Another main consideration, generally omitted, involves the type of firearms used in clay target shooting. For those of a reflective nature, it is probably clear that a gun such as a rifle, firing a single projectile, would hardly be appropriate for hitting a flying target. Obviously, then, a shotgun—which fires a quantity of small lead balls—is the basic firearm for all clay target sports.

Since two distinct (and officially recognized) sports are involved, let's tackle each at a time. Logically, and from an historical standpoint, trapshooting deserves first consideration.

Origins of Trapshooting

Trapshooting traces its origins back to England, in the first quarter of the last century, when a group of country squires devised the idea of augmenting their field shooting by putting live pigeons under a row of old beaver hats to which pieces of string were tied. At the command of "pull," an attendant jerked one of the strings, toppling the hat and releasing the bird. A shooter, stationed at a decorous distance behind the row of hats, attempted to hit the flying bird with his muzzle-loading scattergun.

In due course, the top hats gave way to small iron traps which collapsed, at the jerk of the string, to release the bird—hence the name "trap." The game soon spread to this country and became very popular.

By the end of the 19th century, however, groups, such as the Society for the Prevention of Cruelty to Animals, began to make their voices heard in condemnation of this game. These organizations took a dim view of the wholesale slaughter of pigeons involved—and, to a large degree, popular sentiment agreed. Historically, we have been a nation of sportsmen and the traditions of sport require that game has a fair chance. As a result, while live bird shoots are still held in some parts of this country and abroad, modern trapshooting makes use of inanimate clay targets.

The origins of artificial targets date back to the 1860's when a machine was devised to pitch glass balls through the air in simulation of the flight of live birds. Even though these balls were filled with feathers, to provide a realistic touch when they were hit by a shot charge, they were a poor substitute, in the eyes of the shooters of the day, for hitting a real bird.

Development of Today's Game

By the 1880's, however, a man by the name of George Ligowski had devised something approximating modern clay pigeons. Ligowski's inspiration came from watching small boys skimming clam shells over the water. While his early targets were too fragile and his spring-operated traps for throwing them were rather crude, his idea was the forerunner of modern targets and traps. Better inanimate birds were later devised, along with more sophisticated devices for getting them airborne. In due course specifications for the targets evolved to today's standards which are: diameter 4¼ inches; total height 1-1/16 inches; height from rim 15/32 of an inch; and weight ¾ ounces. Modern targets must be strong enough to withstand the shock of being launched from a spring-operated trap at high speeds, yet fragile enough to break when hit by only three or four pellets of number 7½ shot at 40 yards.

Trapshooting Today

By the early days of this century, trapshooting had developed into essentially its present state. Basically there are three forms of the game: 16 yard shooting, handicap shooting, and doubles. Since all three are shot over the same basic field, a description of the layout is the logical place to start in outlining the sport.

Clay target

A trap field has five shooting stations, located three yards apart, set on a semicircle 16 yards behind a trap house, a low shed-like structure in which an electrically actuated, spring-operated mechanical trap for throwing the birds is located.

Additional shooting stations are located on walkways extending from the 16 yard posts, at intervals of a yard, back to 27 yards. Targets are thrown from the trap at the call of "pull" by each shooter. They fly at varying horizontal angles, but are always going away from the shooter. Vertical angles are constant and the targets, starting out at a rise, gradually fall away, flying a total distance of about 50 to 60 yards from the trap before hitting the ground.

In 16 yard shooting, five people line up, one at each post. Contestants shoot in turn until each has fired at five targets from his initial position. The shooters repeat this procedure, moving to the next station, until all have fired at five targets

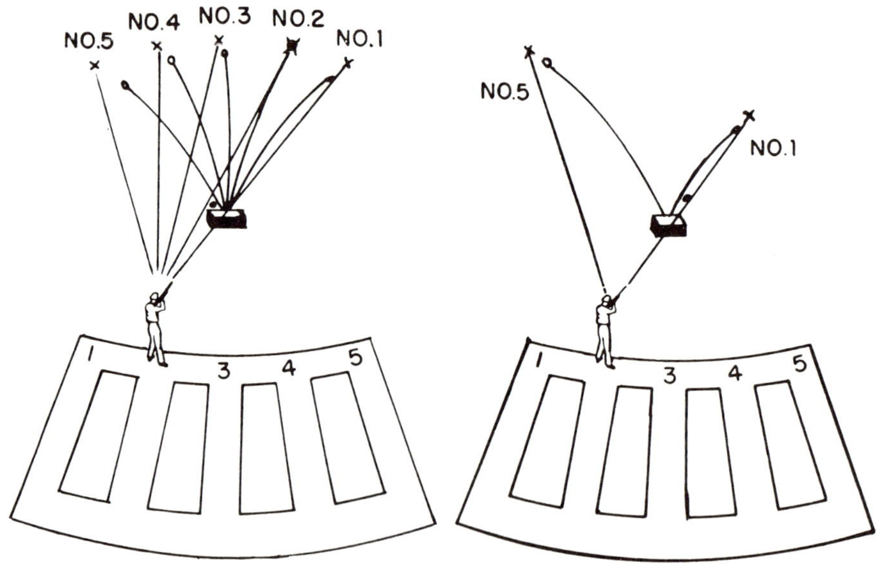

Trap field for singles and doubles

from each position. Thus a complete round consists of 25 targets.

In handicap shooting, the shooters, based on known ability from past performance, shoot from varying yardages. Top flight competitors shoot from 25, 26 or even 27 yards, while those with lower averages are closer to the trap. The course of fire for handicap targets is otherwise identical with that for 16 yard shooting.

In doubles, shooting is done from the 16 yard posts but two targets come out of the house simultaneously on different angles. Skilled doubles shooters generally shoot at the bird flying at the nearest to a straightaway first and then go after the angled target. Top flight trapshooters are generally agreed that doubles is by far the toughest clay target game.

The fundamental principles of the sport of trapshooting, whether targets involved are 16 yard, handicap or doubles, are fairly simple. The shooter is allowed to mount his gun with his cheek firm on the comb of the stock and his eyes looking

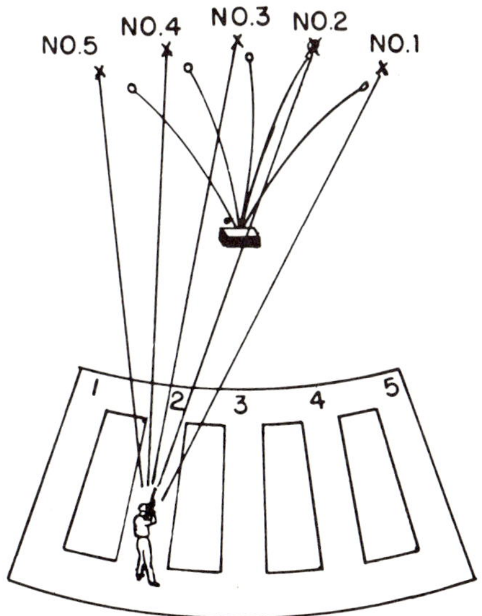

Trap field for handicap shooting

Shooters in position at a trap field

down the barrel—in a completely "ready" position—before he calls for the bird. The target, which is released by an electrical device, flies out almost simultaneously with the call of "pull." The shooter swings his gun along the path of flight of the target, until the muzzle passes the bird, at which point he pulls the trigger. He continues his swing in a smooth, follow-through motion after he has touched off the shot, just as a golfer follows through after hitting the ball. Since target angles may vary from a complete straightaway to an angle of 25 degrees on either side of station number 3 (the center post on the field), it's clear that some shots require more "lead" than others. This is particularly true when shooting is done from handicap yardages. The basic principles of lead as described in Chapter 6 apply to trapshooting as well as to all other phases of the shotgun sports.

Trap Guns

While almost any 12 gauge shotgun can be used at trap, as long as it has a full or modified choke barrel, specialized firearms are available. Anyone seriously interested in the sport would be advised to purchase a shotgun designed for the game.

Pump actions, autoloaders, over-and-under doubles, side-by-side doubles and single-shot guns are all used. Obviously a double or a repeater is necessary for doubles shooting where two shots are required.

Since all trapshooting is done with 12 gauge guns, specialized trap guns, of whatever action style, are all 12 bore. The main differences, between a field grade scattergun and one designed for trap, are in the stock dimensions and the barrel. Trap stocks are much straighter than standard because a straight stock makes it easier to mount the gun comfortably for targets that are all "going away" at a constant vertical

Typical trap guns. Pump action above, automatic below

angle. In addition, stocks are generally fitted with a rubber recoil pad which not only eases recoil effect on the shoulder in long races, but helps to prevent the butt from slipping from the shoulder once it is put there.

Barrels are usually 28 or more inches long and are fitted with ventilated ribs. Barrels of this length give a better sighting plane for more accurate pointing. Ventilated ribs also improve the sighting plane, giving the shooter an even surface the entire length of the barrel.

Trap guns are generally full choke although some shooters do use tight-shooting, modified barrels. As we have seen, a full choke gun is designed to put 70 percent or more of the shot in a 30 inch circle at 40 yards. Since the average distance at which trap targets are broken is about 40 yards from the gun, a tight pattern at this distance is necessary.

When autoloading shotguns are used for trap, they should be fitted with a deflector to prevent ejected shells from flying into the face of the shooter on the next station. All standard autoloaders, made in this country for trapshooting, are so equipped.

Ammunition

The rules of trapshooting state that the maximum load permitted in competition may have no more than 3 drams equivalent of powder and no more than 1⅛ ounces of shot. The largest shot size permitted is 7½. The major ammunition companies manufacture loads, conforming to these specifications, that are specially designed for trapshooting.

The Amateur Trapshooting Association

The governing body, for organized trapshooting in this country, is the Amateur Trapshooting Association with headquarters in Vandalia, Ohio. Registered shoots are conducted all over the country under ATA auspices. These include state and regional championships as well as local club shoots. The "World Series" of trapshooting, the "Grand American," is held every summer on the ATA's home grounds at Vandalia. In the main event, the "Grand American" Handicap, more than 2,000 contestants test their skill for prizes that run into thousands of dollars.

Whether a shooter's objective is top flight competition in registered tournaments or just an afternoon's fun at the local gun club, trapshooting can provide lots of thrills and good sport. Trapshooters are a friendly bunch and most gun clubs are glad to help beginners.

Skeet Shooting

Compared to its big brother, trapshooting, skeet is a relative baby. Its origins date back to about 1915 when a group of sportsmen decided to try to devise a clay target game that offered shooting situations more closely approximating those encountered in upland game hunting.

Their first attempt was a game called "clock shooting" in which shooting posts were located on the perimeter of a circle around a standard trap. The various stations offered shots at targets from all angles; outgoers, incomers, crossing and quartering.

Refinements of the Game

In time the game was refined to its present form by installation of two traps—one in a high house and the other in a low house—which face each other. Seven shooting stations are equally spaced between the two on a semi-circle with the first at the high house and the seventh at the low. An eighth post is located on a line halfway between the two houses. In a standard round of skeet, the shooter starts at Station #1 and shoots at a target from the high house. He then calls for a bird from the low house. He repeats this procedure at each station around the field. The targets always fly on the same path and varying angles are achieved by moving from one station to another. At station #8, the one located between the two trap houses, the targets fly almost directly over the shooter's head and he must break them before they pass the center position of the field.

After touring the field once, shooting single targets as described above, the shooter returns to Station #1 for his doubles. Two targets are thrown simultaneously, one from the high house and one from the low. The shooter tries to break the bird going away first and then goes after the incomer. This procedure is repeated at Stations #2, #6 and #7. If the shooter has broken all of the targets thrown, up until this point, he may take his 25th or optional shot, from any point that he desires. If he misses a bird earlier in the round, he repeats that target immediately. As in trapshooting, one round consists of 25 targets.

Growth of the Sport

The first skeet field was installed by Charles E. Davies, and some friends, at the Glen Rock Kennels near Reading, Mass. For a number of years, the game was limited to this one field. Then, in 1926, the late William H. Foster, editor of the *National Sportsmen* and *Hunting and Fishing* magazines, published stories about the layout in both publications. Foster, because of the work he did in promoting and refining the sport, is often called the "father of skeet." In addition to his promotional efforts, he also helped to christen the game, which had been nameless until that point. Over 10,000 entries

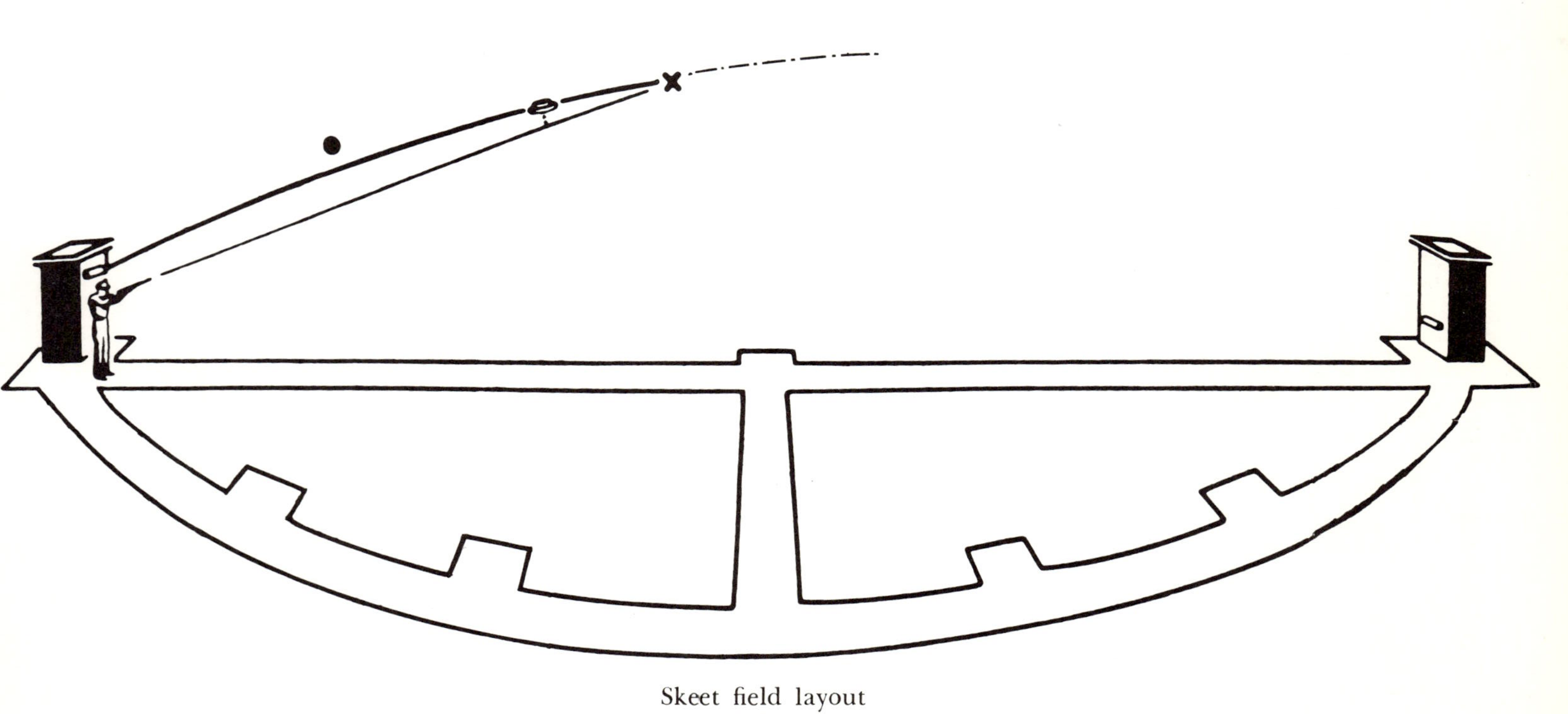

Skeet field layout

were received in a contest he ran to find the best name. The winner, "skeet," which is an old Scandinavian word meaning "shoot," was submitted by Mrs. Gertrude Hulbert of Dayton, Montana.

Skeet caught on quickly after that. Within the next few years thousands of skeet clubs were organized or layouts were installed at existing gun clubs. The National Skeet Shooting Association was organized as the governing body for the sport. Today, registered tournaments, including the National Championships, are held under the auspices of the NSSA, which has its headquarters in Dallas, Texas, in much the same manner as trapshooting competition is handled by the Amateur Trapshooting Association.

The Game Today

Skeet today is one of our fastest growing participant sports. Competitions are held for four different gauges of shotguns, the .410, 28, 20 and 12, and the larger tournaments include events for all four guns.

Originally, the rules of the game required that shooters keep the gun butt below the waist when calling for the bird and there was a variation of up to three seconds between the time the shooter called "pull" and the time the target was thrown. (The target could come out immediately or it might be delayed up to 3 seconds.) In international competition, these rules still apply, but under the rules for competition in this country, the gun may now be mounted to the shoulder, before calling for the bird, and targets are thrown instantaneously. In order to be sure that the puller knows which bird (high house or low house) the shooter is calling for, the call of "pull" is supposed to be used for the high house and "mark" for the low house.

Since target flight varies from straightaways at Stations #1

Action at station #2 on a skeet field

and #7, to shots that are at right angles, at Station #4, and incomers at Station #8, skeet fulfills its original intent of offering shooting situations more closely paralleling those found in hunting. The arguments among scattergunners who favor skeet over trap (or vice versa), about which game is harder, are legion. The trap fan claims that the unknown angles, at which his targets fly, provide more of an element of surprise—and thus require more skill—while the skeet addict believes the wider variety of angles—even if known—are more challenging. There are a number of shooters who are proficient at and enjoy both games. For here, suffice it is to say that both are great sport.

Skeet Guns

Any good upland shotgun can be used at skeet, provided the shooter is not out to win any major trophies. Because the average distance at which targets are broken is about 20 yards, the gun should have an open bore, which will deliver its most effective pattern at this distance.

Just as the trap shooter goes in for specially designed shotguns, so does the skeet fan. Stock dimensions of skeet guns are the same as those for field shooting—the straight stock of the trap gun would actually be a handicap. Barrels are usually 26 inches long, making for faster pointing at the relatively short ranges involved in skeet. Most gun manufacturers offer barrels with special "skeet" choke which gives a slightly tighter pattern than a plain, open-cylinder bore. Ventilated ribs on the barrels are preferred because they offer an even sighting plane.

Obviously, because of the requirements of the "doubles" phase of the game, skeet guns must be capable of firing two shots in rapid succession. Autoloaders, pumps, over-and-under doubles and side-by-side doubles, are all popular. In recent years, the autoloaders have come into greater and greater favor —particularly the gas-operated models. Because these guns vent off some of the gas to operate the action, they are far lighter in recoil effect than fixed action models. In addition. they are fast pointing, easy handling, and they are capable of firing two shots just as fast as the shooter can pull the trigger. As an example of their popularity, more autoloaders are seen at most of the big shoots these days than all other styles combined.

The pumps and doubles still have their strong advocates, however, and many top flight shooters use them very effectively. In the last analysis, all four styles can do the job and it comes down to a matter of shooter preference.

How to Shoot Skeet

The basic fundamentals of lead and form described in Chapter 6 apply to skeet just as much as they do to trap. Lead, again, is the key to success. More targets are missed in both games, because the shooter shoots behind them, than for any other reason. As is the case with trapshooting, there are those who try to estimate the distance a shooter must shoot ahead of a target in order to hit it. Many of these people are eminent authorities on the sport and excellent shots.

Such considerations can be confusing to the beginner, however. The secret of success is the idea of "swing and follow through."

In addition to the analogies of the football player, the man with the garden hose and the golfer discussed earlier, let's introduce a new character, a tennis player, to help further explain this theory. In hitting a golf shot, the player keeps his head down and his eyes on the ball. When he swings the club, he continues to look at the ball, and *after hitting it,* he continues his swing in a smooth follow through. If he tried to stop his swing at the moment of contact with the ball, he wouldn't have much luck. By the same token, the tennis player keeps his eyes on the ball—not the racket—and after hitting his shot, he continues to swing his racket in a smooth follow through. Without this follow through, his shot would pop up in the air and go nowhere, except in the case of a volley at the net.

A shotgun shooter, whether he is on a skeet or trap field or after game, must follow the same principle. First of all, he looks at the target over his barrel, not at the barrel. In the second place, he must follow through in a smooth continuous motion, after touching off his shot.

As we pointed out earlier, it is obvious that the target must be lead. The greater the angle, the greater the lead. By swinging the gun along the flight path of the target, pulling the trigger as the target is passed, and following through, the shooter automatically calculates lead. He swing faster for the right or left angle than the straightaway, thus making his lead longer when it is necessary.

In the last analysis the best way to learn any sport is to go out and try it. Most gun clubs welcome beginners and will be glad to help them out. It's wise to start out with a good instructor so that the fundamentals can be learned properly at the start.

Ammunition for Skeet

As was pointed out earlier, four gauges of guns are used in skeet. The rules of the game specify that guns and ammunition in each gauge meet the following requirements:

.410—(or sub-small bore)—Requires a gun of 410 gauge and shot of no more than ½ ounce no smaller than size 9

28 (or small bore)—Requires a gun of 28 gauge (or smaller) and restricts shot charge to ¾ of an ounce not smaller than size 9

20 gauge—Requires a gun of 20 gauge (or smaller) and restricts the shot size to 7/8 of an ounce not smaller than size 9

All-Bore—Permits the use of a gun up to and including 12 gauge and restricts the shot charge to 1 1/8 ounces not smaller than size 9

There are also requirements for maximum powder charges for each gauge. The ammunition companies all manufacture special shells designed for skeet shooting which meet these specifications.

In summary, the clay target sports, both trap and skeet, offer the field shooter an excellent means of sharpening his eye for hunting. More important, perhaps, both games are organized, recognized sports which offer good competition and plenty of fun for contestants.

CHAPTER 8

Upland Hunting

There is a vast difference between shooting at an inanimate target on a trap or skeet field and facing a fast-flushing game bird in the field. A grouse, exploding unexpectedly from the leaves, or a covey of quail leaping skyward from close cover can be disconcerting, even to the experienced hunter.

The elements of proper gun handling apply equally in all shotgunning situations, however. Whether the target is animate or inanimate, you must still follow the swing and follow through principles outlined earlier, if you expect success from your efforts.

Hand Traps and Quail Walks

Game birds are unpredictable critters. They seldom appear at just the moment you want them to and when they do decide to fly, they have a way of heading somewhere other than the direction you expect them to take. Obviously that is what makes upland hunting fun—and sport! While formal trap and skeet shooting are good training in the basics of how to hit flying targets, they do not necessarily prepare hunters for the unexpected situations found in the field. There are several clay target games that can help, however. Hand traps, which are small portable devices for throwing clay targets, can be carried anywhere. Two people, one the thrower and the other the shooter, can get invaluable hunting warm-up experience with these gadgets. Targets can be thrown at almost any

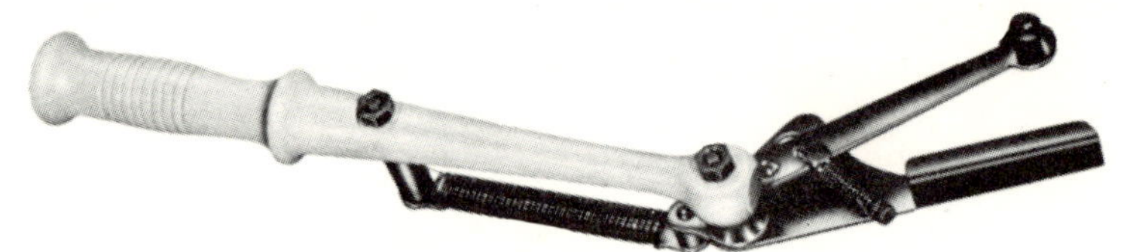

A hand trap

angle or height, and in all kinds of cover, so it is possible to simulate almost any hunting situation.

Quail walks and tower shoots are also good practice. In these, clay targets are thrown under conditions approximating field situations as closely as possible. The shooter doesn't know when the target will appear or, often, where.

In the last analysis, though, there is no artificial substitute for the real thing. Once the fundamentals of shotgun handling have been learned, you are ready to face the joys and frustrations of going afield.

Types of Upland Game

The almost infinite variety of upland game makes any attempt to describe the various species, in a blanket definition, very difficult. In the first place, the names themselves are confusing. For example our quail bear little relationship to the bird known by the same name in Europe. European quail, which resemble our meadow larks, are migratory birds while our species tend to live out their lives in one general area.

The confusion derives from the fact that the first settlers on this continent tended to give names to native birds based on even vague similarities to the species they had known at home. Not being ornithologists, they often made mistakes. Thus six different birds in this country are known as "quail."

In general there are three types of upland game birds in

North America. The first are Galliformes, the second are Culumbiformes, and the third are Limicolae.

The vast majority of hunted species, including pheasants, partridge, quail, turkeys and grouse (sometimes incorrectly called partridge) are Galliformes. Culumbiformes are all of the pigeon and dove clan. Limicolae include all manner of so-called "shore birds" such as sandpipers, plovers, yellow legs and curlews as well as two species classed as game birds; the jacksnipe and the woodcock.

Within each of these major groups there are various sub-species. Let's look at Galliformes first. In the case of turkeys, the recognized types include the Eastern, the Florida, the Mid-western, the Western and the Mexican.

Grouse include sage hens, blue grouse, prairie chickens, sharp-tailed grouse, Franklins grouse, ruffed grouse, spruce hens, and ptarmigan. The partridge family embraces Hungarians, Francolins and chukars. The quail clan includes the standard bobwhite, valley quail, mountain quail, Gambels quail, scaled quail and Mearns's (Harlequin) quail.

Pheasants, which are not native American birds but were imported from China, include the standard ring-necked, which has taken hold in large numbers all over the Northern half of the country; and the Reeves pheasant, a more recent import from the Far East.

Among the most famed of the Culumbiformes are the now extinct passenger pigeons. Hunters have often been accused of causing the demise of these birds but modern authorities are fairly well agreed that the real villain was the march of civilization. Others of this family hunted today include the mourning dove and the white-winged dove.

A number of small animals are also classed as upland game. Chief among these are rabbits and squirrels. As is the case with upland birds, there are numerous sub-species of each. The rabbit clan includes the standard cottontail as well as his larger cousins the jack rabbit and the snowshoe (or varying hare). Squirrels include greys and reds plus a number of other types.

Animals such as fox, though sometimes hunted with shotguns, are really more accurately classified as varmints.

Some larger game animals, such as black bear and deer, are occasionally hunted with shotguns loaded with rifled slugs or buckshot. A later chapter will deal with this subject in more detail.

The Gun For the Game

In earlier chapters we have reviewed the design characteristics and uses for the myriad different shotgun styles, gauges and barrel lengths. Specifications of various types of ammunition have also been covered. As we have seen, hard and fast rules are not necessarily applicable. In many cases, the choice is based more on personal preference and prejudice than on any reasoned argument. In truth, modern shotguns and shotgun shells are so efficient that almost any combination of the two is capable of taking game, provided the hunter has acquired the basic skills necessary.

It is obvious, however, that larger gauge guns and larger shot sizes are best suited for bigger birds and animals. However, recent improvements in the design of guns and the ballistic efficiency of ammunition, have narrowed the gap between the 12 and the 20 gauge. With magnum loads and full choke barrels, the lighter, faster-handling 20's can turn in creditable performances (even at pass shooting for waterfowl). Actually, they can almost match standard loads in 12's. With some hunters, as a result, it becomes a matter of pride to achieve success with the smaller gauge guns.

Perhaps the most important consideration, in the choice of gauge and shell, is the conditions that exist in the area you plan to hunt. If your quarry is pheasant in open areas or grouse in heavy cover, the 12 is probably your best bet. If you are also a waterfowl hunter, the choice is doubly apt. If you are after quail, woodcock or other smaller birds, an open choke 12 or a 20 may well do the trick. In the last analysis, your best guide is experience.

Hunting With a Dog

Perhaps one of the greatest joys of upland hunting is going afield with a well-trained dog. The breed isn't important as long as it is a hunting species. The mere fact it is of the canine clan gives it a vast advantage over poor homo sapiens. A dog can find, flush and retrieve game that a man might otherwise never even see. This last point is perhaps the most important. For the true sportsman, there is no greater sin than downing a bird or animal and failing to pick it up.

Having one or more dogs afield may create some problems, however. The degree of training is obviously vital. A green pup may not hold his point steadily, resulting in game flushing before the hunter is ready. A shot under these circumstances can be dangerous since you run the risk of hitting the dog. Proper handling is also necessary. Above all remember that if the dog isn't yours, let his owner work him. Extra orders from others in the party will only confuse the animal. Remember also that a retriever will fetch game to his master, not necessarily to the hunter who downed the bird.

For upland hunting, setters and pointers are the most popular species. However, retrievers and spaniels are also used. The famed beagles (and other trailing hounds) are designed for small game such as rabbits, though they will occasionally flush birds for the alert hunter.

A hunter and his dog

Fashions for the Field

It is important to dress for the activity, no matter what the sport you engage in. It is not necessary to go afield looking like a fashion advertisement but it is vital to wear clothes that are practical. Perhaps the first consideration is to be sure you're neither too hot nor too cold. Determine the temperatures you can expect before you start out and dress accordingly. Equal in importance is the need to keep dry. You may not run into wet weather but it is well to be prepared. There is nothing more miserable than being caught far from your base of operations in a downpour, without the proper gear.

Good hunting boots are vital. They should be sufficiently waterproof to keep you dry, and sturdy enough to permit you to go through heavy cover. Your trousers, too, should be tough enough so that they are not easily ripped by snags. Leg protectors or heavy leather boots are important if you are in an area where poisonous snakes might be a problem.

In upland hunting, where you walk through woods and fields, often in heavy cover, it is important to wear some bright colored clothing. The standard olive-drab garb of the duck hunter may cause problems for other hunters—and you! No one wants to be mistaken for a bird or animal as he moves through the brush, but, unfortunately such things have happened with disastrous results for all concerned.

A good hunting coat, with adequate pockets for ammunition and downed game, is also important.

Field Shooting

One of the prime rules of upland hunting is GO SLOWLY. If you set too fast a pace, you may charge right past game holding in close cover without ever seeing it. Wild creatures depend on protective colors as one of their main defenses against predators of all kinds. True, if you have a dog with you, he will use his nose to find game you would never discover, but there are occasions when you may flush a bird or rabbit your dog has passed by. If you are going too fast, you will never get a chance at a shot.

Once you are afield, you must always be ready for anything. Common sense dictates that you keep the safety of your gun on until you want to shoot, but you should carry your gun in a position that permits you to throw it to your shoulder, flick off the safety and fire, in almost a reflex motion. Obviously, you must be sure of your target before shooting at anything but it does pay to practice the business of getting a shot off quickly when the opportunity presents itself. Carry your gun pointing down or in an across-the-chest position and keep your trigger finger outside the guard but near it (and the safety).

Remember that game likes relatively protected spots such as field edges, brush patches, hollows, and areas of second growth woods. Birds and animals don't often get caught in the open where they have little chance of getting to cover quickly. Kick the brush piles and clumps of grass and weeds as you go by. You never know what might be there.

Field Etiquette

Hunting is a companionable sport. It's much more fun to hunt with a friend than by yourself. As is the case with any activity involving more than one person, however, you have to think about your partners and observe some basic rules of courtesy.

Common sense is the prime dictate of hunting etiquette. Couple this with the golden rule and you will have it made. Remember that a hunting trip is not designed to prove who is the best shot or who can fill his bag first. Set down some

He brings them in with pride

guide lines before you start and the day will be more fun for all.

Decide on shooting areas and stick to them. If you and your friend are walking abreast down a corn field, make sure the shooter on the left takes only birds flushing to his side and the shooter on the right those on his. For birds coming straight in or going straight away, alternate the shooting order. If three hunters are abreast, the middle man takes the incomers and outgoers and those on the sides go after the ones on their edges.

There is no greater sin, nor any quicker way to estrange yourself from the group, than to claim birds you have not actually hit. True, there may be situations where two hunters shoot almost simultaneously and it is hard to say who made the kill. It is far better to go through an Alfonse and Gaston routine and keep a friend than to assert your rights and maybe lose one. If you do miss, don't wail about it. The best of shots have their off days but, if they are real sportsmen, they accept their slumps with good grace.

Make sure you shoot only at birds or animals within range. It may build up your ego to scratch down a pheasant with three or four pellets at 60 yards but your chances of doing so are remote. Actually you run the risk of crippling, and not killing, the bird. It may then run or fly off only to die later; a tragic loss to conservation and good sportsmanship.

Be sure you know where all of the other members of your party are at all times. Both safety and courtesy dictate this rule. Always control the direction in which your gun muzzle is pointing so that if it should go off accidentally, you won't hurt anyone, including yourself.

Farmer-Sportsman Relations

We live in an age of increasing urbanization of our open land areas. While much work is being done, by private and

Hunting is a companionable sport

public agencies, to insure that we preserve our remaining wilderness for posterity, most upland hunting today is done on agricultural lands. For this reason, there has never been a time in our history when good relations between farmers and sportsmen were more important.

It is bad enough to drive up to an area you knew, from several years ago, as good open land and find it filled with a housing development or a shopping center. It is far worse, however, to find it still good hunting land but posted with a sign saying: "Keep off. No hunting or fishing." When this happens, it is all too often the fault of thoughtless people who have failed to respect the farmer's property.

Put yourself in the position of the landowner. Suppose you had given a group of hunters permission to use your land. And then, suppose you found that they had left gates open permitting your stock animals to wander; had left picnic lunch litter in your fields; had trampled across newly plowed or seeded land; had used your fence posts for targets; or (and it has happened) had killed one of your domestic birds or animals, mistaking it for game. Chances are you would be pretty mad about the whole thing. Let it happen two or three times and our friend the farmer says: "The heck with the whole business" and puts up a sign.

None of this is necessary, however. If sportsmen would observe a few simple rules, most landowners would welcome them. The first rule is *ask permission*. Nothing is better calculated to arouse a farmer's ire than to find people whom he has never seen making themselves at home in his fields. Second in importance is the idea of thinking of the other fellow. Don't leave gates open, don't leave litter in fields, don't take pot shots at fence posts (or buildings), don't walk across plowed fields, and ABOVE ALL observe the rules of common courtesy you would expect of any guest on your own property. When the hunt is over, offer to share some of your game with the landowner. He may not accept but he'll be flattered that you thought of him. Better still, next time you want to hunt on his land, bring him a small gift as an expression of your thanks for his friendliness.

Hunting For a Fee

The sheer pressure of hunting near urban areas, where most of our population is concentrated these days, has resulted in some new solutions to the problems of landowner-sportsman relations. In some parts of the country, farmers have come to recognize game for the valuable asset it is. By leasing hunting rights to sportsmen's clubs, and then planting the necessary feed on fallow lands, they have been able to enhance the game supply and pay for it. The fees must be reasonable or the idea won't work. State and Federal agencies are equipped to assist landowners interested in arrangements of this type.

Shooting preserves are another answer to the problem. In these operations, game birds such as pheasants, quail, chukars, partridge, and sometimes mallard ducks are pen raised. They are then released for specific parties of hunters in land areas that offer natural cover and habitat. The birds are put out well before the hunting party arrives and conditions are as sporting as you could want. Hunters pay for the game released but many of these birds escape to the wild to enhance the breeding population.

A majority of states now permit and encourage preserve hunting. The basic guide lines laid down for this type of operation insure that the sport can rival the best to be found for wild birds. The proximity of most of these areas to large cities makes it possible for the urban dweller to find good hunting within easy reach of his home.

CHAPTER 9

Waterfowl Hunting

The waterfowl found in North America can be broken down into three main categories: ducks, geese, and swans. All of them are members of the *Anatidae* family and they share the common characteristics of having webbed feet, flat bills, longish necks, and rather short tails. In addition they are amphibious critters; not very happy for too long when they are away from water.

Within these three broad groups, there are 48 sub-species whose individual traits and habits are extremely varied. Some like big, open water and others prefer secluded, wooded ponds. Some are as bright hued as an Elizabethan dandy and others are as drab as a Grant Wood farm wife. Their sizes range from the giants of the swan clan to the tiny teals. A mixed chorus of their voices would surpass the range of the most grandiose cast at the Metropolitan Opera.

Of the three main categories, the swans are the most distinctive. Though sometimes considered game birds, they have not been legally hunted, except for a limited season on whistling swans in Utah, in recent years, since the ratification of the Migratory Bird Treaty between the United States and Canada in 1918. All swans found in North America are large white birds with very long necks. The commonest and the biggest are whistling swans whose range extends to both coasts. So-called mute swans, a European import, are somewhat smaller. Trumpeters, the third type, are native to this continent.

Geese range in size between swans and ducks. The commonest members of this family are the Canadas, found all over the continent. A favorite of hunters, these birds have eleven sub-species ranging from the small cackling Canadas of the Pacific coast to the giant Canadas whose range covers parts of the midwest. All of these birds have black heads and necks and white spots on their cheeks. Essentially grain eaters, Canadas tend to feed in corn fields although they like to rest on or near water.

Blue and snow geese are first cousins and in appearance and habits they share many traits. Size and color are their chief differentiating characteristics. Current theories are that the greater snows are the parents of the type and that the blues are mutations of the lesser snows. The mutation theory is borne out by the fact that lesser snows and blues are often found in the same flocks. The range of all three types is almost as wide as the Canadas.

White-fronted geese are a more localized species. They favor the wide open spaces of the West. A favorite of gourmets, they are regarded as true table delicacies.

The last three types of geese are brant, Ross' Geese and emperors. Brant are basically sea birds. They feed on eelgrass and sea lettuce and are found on both coasts. The emperors, also sea lovers, are mainly Alaskan birds, seldom seen in most flyways of this country. Ross' geese are relatively small birds, sometimes confused with snows because of their white color. Most of these birds migrate south through California.

The duck family, the largest of the waterfowl clan, divides into some 37 species. Detailed classification of this armada is a difficult task at best. Basically, however, they break down into two main groups, the "Puddle ducks" (or "dabblers") and the diving ducks which favor deeper water. The "dabblers," which include mallards, pintails, blacks, teal, widgeon, wood, and mottled, like shallow ponds and marshes.

Redheads and canvasbacks are the best known of the divers. Underwater feeders, they seldom forage in crop fields. For

Canada geese come in to rest, Lake Manitoba

nesting sites, they prefer the prairie "potholes" of Manitoba, Saskatchewan and the North Central States. Other birds in this group are the greater and less scaup and ringnecks.

A third group are the mergansers. Their principal food is aquatic animals. Sometimes known as "fish ducks" they are scorned by many as table fare because their marine diet carries over into their taste when cooked.

Ruddy ducks are a sub-species all by themselves. Divers by nature, they feed on plants rather than fish. Tree ducks, largely limited to the Gulf Coast, have long legs and relatively small bodies.

Other marsh birds, such as clapper and sora rail, though not of the Anatidae clan, are also prized by waterfowl hunters. Unlike upland birds, which are apt to live out their lives in relatively limited areas, most waterfowl are migratory. They nest in the northern parts of the North American continent and winter in warmer climates, some as far away as South America. They are hunted chiefly during the period of their migration in the fall. In northern states and Canada, the seasons open in September or October and keep on until November or December. Further south, the seasons may not open until November or December and they may run into January.

Because of their migratory nature, waterfowl are truly an international wildlife resource. Proper waterfowl management requires the cooperation of Canadian authorities, who control the major nesting areas, and various state and Federal authorities in this country. Master plans for seasons and bag limits are made each year under the terms of a treaty between the two countries.

Waterfowl flyways of North America

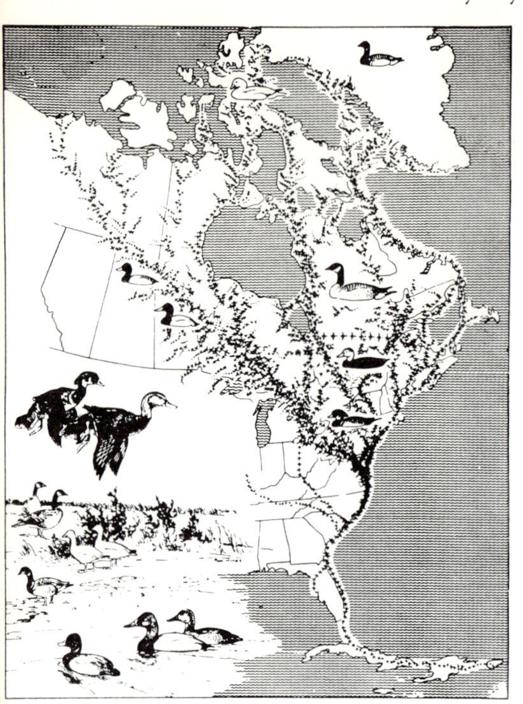

Atlantic Flyway

Mississippi Flyway

Central Flyway

Pacific Flyway

The Four Flyways

Waterfowl are basically creatures of habit and their behavior patterns are passed on from generation to generation. By some miraculous instinct, birds hatched in one area tend to go back to the same spot to nest the next year, after their winter vacations. The mystery of how they solve this complex navigation problem, in flights North and South of thousands of miles, has never been mastered by man. They have been doing this since long before Columbus and they need neither a compass nor a sextant to accomplish their objectives.

Waterfowl, on this continent, tend to migrate in four main flight patterns, known as "flyways." From East to West, these are: the Atlantic, the Mississippi, the Central and the Pacific. There is some overlap in the areas from which these flights start and end. The central point, from which some birds fan East, some West and some down the middle, are the Canadian prairie provinces of Manitoba and Saskatchewan (and to a lesser extent, their Southern counterparts in the midwestern part of the United States). The maps shown on page 92 show this graphically far more effectively than can be described in words.

Conservation Problems

More than any other species of wildlife, waterfowl populations are at the mercy of conditions in their basic nesting areas. A drought in the prairie provinces can dry up thousands of "potholes," used for nesting and the rearing of young, with dire effects. Extend the drought for two, three or more years and the results can border on catastrophe. The inexorable march of agriculture can be equally disastrous. Waterfowl need water and plenty of it to produce new birds. In the case of

Log Valley pothole development, South Saskatchewan

Swift current key waters, South Saskatchewan

many species, the favored production areas are the small farm ponds and "potholes" so prevalent in Central Canada and the North Central part of the United States. When farmers drain these areas, to produce more agricultural land, as they have been doing for years, vital nesting areas are lost forever.

A number of private and public agencies are hard at work trying to alleviate this problem. Federal funds are available, as a result of the sale of duck stamps (all waterfowl hunters must purchase these each year) and other programs in the conservation field. These funds are used to buy up marginal agricultural lands, which offer good nesting facilities, to preserve them for waterfowl production. The Canadian Government is also taking some concrete steps in this area.

Private groups such as Ducks Unlimited, an organization of hunters and sportsmen, are also playing a vital part in solving this problem. Funds collected by DU are used, almost entirely, in work designed to preserve and improve nesting areas in Canada.

Much remains to be done, however, and it behooves every duck hunter and lover of waterfowl to do everything in his power to preserve not only nesting areas but nesting spots along the flyways and in the wintering grounds. Without such activities waterfowl, and the sport of hunting these birds, is doomed.

One encouraging sign in this picture, is the adaptability of some species. Wildlife management experts have had a fair degree of success in establishing nesting flocks of mallards, Canada geese, and other species, on a local basis all over this country. By providing proper habitat and releasing hatchery raised birds or birds with clipped wings that will raise their young locally, it has been possible to develop waterfowl that stay in the areas where they were born for generation after generation. Not all species are adaptable to this sort of management, but for those that are, this practice offers some real promise.

Oakland Lakes project, South Alberta

Fortunately, for the future of waterfowl and the sport of waterfowl hunting, sportsmen are among those most interested in the conservation problems involved. They are in the forefront of groups dedicated to preserving habitat and maintaining sound and reasonable regulations. They cooperate wholeheartedly with Federal and international organizations charged with the responsibility of setting seasons and bag limits. With the support of all these groups, the waterfowl situation can improve vastly, in spite of the encroachments of civilization, in the years to come.

Waterfowl Blinds

Waterfowl hunting is a far more sedentary sport than the pursuit of upland game. Because the areas in which these birds are found are limited to marshes, small ponds, estuaries, rivers and the in-shore areas of larger bodies of water, it is possible to hunt them in relatively restricted locales. This very restriction poses some special problems, however. You can't get any closer to the birds than to put yourself in the general area where you know they are located. After that, the problem becomes one of getting them to come to you.

The first thing to remember is that waterfowl have keen eyes. Often they can spot you long before you can see them. It is thus apparent that one of the first rules for this type of hunting is to keep out of sight. If you are hunting diving ducks in open water areas, this may involve finding a rocky area where you can get down out of view. Or it may mean using a duck boat and lying flat on the bottom of it until the birds are in range. In marsh areas or in hunting on small ponds and rivers, it means building a blind out of the natural growth of the locale to keep yourself hidden.

For goose hunting in cornfields, it involves the construction of a cornstalk concealment area or the digging of a pit, lined with a concrete culvert pipe or an old barrel, into which you can lower yourself to keep out of sight. Illustrations of some typical waterfowl blinds, showing their construction are shown on pages 98 and 99. The chief consideration is to build a blind that blends into the area as naturally as possible. Once the structure is completed, get in it and stay in it until the birds are in range. The slightest movement of a gun or the tilting of your face skyward at the wrong moment can spook birds long before they are near enough to shoot.

Dress For The Sport

Proper clothes are as much a part of the business of staying concealed as is a good blind. Bright colors are definitely out and the waterfowler's garb must blend with the natural background as closely as possible. The standard olive drab, or even camouflaged clothing, work best. A hat of similar color is also important.

Weatherproof clothing is also vital. For some types of

Geese blind using portable cornstalks

An easy blind to set up

hunting, where it is necessary to do some wading to get to a blind, hip boots or even waders are a must. In other areas, a good pair of rubber boots will do the trick. Since ducks and geese love wet and inclement weather, you'll want clothes that will keep you dry and warm. A good set of long woolies or thermal underwear, a woolen shirt and a warm sweater topped with proper boots and water resistant olive drab pants and jacket are standard. If the day is warm, you can omit some of the underpinnings. If it is wet, you will probably want a set of foul weather gear with a hooded parka as an extra adjunct. Any good sporting goods store can help you with the proper gear for the locale you will be in.

Decoys

Years ago, waterfowl hunters used to trap live birds and tie them up, outside of their blinds, to attract other birds within shooting range. The dictates of good sportsmanship, backed up by stringent regulations forbidding the practice, have made such live decoys a thing of the past, and rightly so. There's no doubt that they worked! The problem was they worked too well and tipped the balance too far in favor of the hunter!

Carved or molded decoys are another matter, however. They are a vital and fascinating adjunct to waterfowling. The art of carving and painting such replicas of live birds, in as realistic a fashion as possible, has a long and honoured history. Collectors of Americana prize some of the decoys made years ago and the work of the best decoy makers of several generations past is as revered among duck hunting purists as are the paintings of the best of the American primitives, among art collectors. Today, carefully carved and painted decoys are prized as book ends or mantel piece decorations.

Good serviceable decoys today are molded in a variety of synthetic materials, as well as carved, and they must be

Decoys in position

realistic enough to attract birds. The secret of using them properly is in setting them out. Study the habits of ducks in the area you are hunting and try to place your decoys accordingly. Watch the wind direction and study the location of natural feed. Remember that ducks and geese tend to land coming into the wind, just as an airplane does. Try to put out your spread in as natural a posture as possible.

Waterfowl Retrievers

A good dog is equally as necessary to waterfowl hunting as to the pursuit of upland game. Dogs of the retriever species such as Labradors, Chesapeakes and Goldens are favored, although some of the spaniel clan are also good. A description of the proper training of these dogs is beyond the scope of this book. The important thing to remember is that waterfowl, obviously, are most often hunted over water. A good dog is vital to pick up birds that land in areas too deep to be retrieved by wading. In addition, a retriever can penetrate marsh areas and heavy cover to find downed birds or cripples that might otherwise never be picked up. As in the case with upland game, it is the mark of a good sportsman and a true conservationist to hunt with a dog.

Calls

The art of calling game bears some relationship to the skill of a good cook. Some people have it, others do not. In the James Bay area of Canada, Cree Indian guides, practicing an art as old as time, call geese with no artificial aids at all. Old time guides on the Eastern shore of the Chesapeake Bay can fool the wiliest Canada Geese the same way. Today, however, it is not necessary to be a Pied Piper. Artificial calls, which are actuated with lung power, are available and, with

Retriever at work

a bit of practice, anyone can learn to use them. True success in waterfowling requires the use of a call just as much as it involves proper blinds and clothing. One of the true joys of the sport is found in the ability to turn a passing flight of birds with a call and bring them back towards your spread of decoys.

Typical Duck and Goose calls from left to right. The Marble Arms Duck call, Herters Goose Call, Herters Duck Call, Abercrombie & Fitch Deluxe Duck Call, Abercrombie & Fitch Duck Call, L. L. Beane Duck Call, Olt Rubber Duck Call, The Olt Magnum Duck Call. The decoy is George Soules medium height head coastal deluxe black duck decoy.

In recent years, some actual recordings of the sounds of ducks and geese have been made. Federal law forbids the use of these records for hunting but the neophyte who wants to learn how to use a mouth call can find them of vast benefit as a learning aid.

Make Sure They Are In Range

One of the greatest sins of some waterfowlers, as well as upland hunters, is "skybusting." Whether it is the excitement of the moment or just plain lack of knowledge, they tend to shoot at birds way out of range. Every hunter has heard of kills supposedly made at 70 or 80 yards. The simple truth is, however, that such shots are almost impossible. Once in a while a few pellets may reach out that far and knock down a bird but when this happens it is largely luck. The effective range of a shotgun—even a full choke with magnum loads—is not much more than 60 yards and shots at this range are risky. Most clean kills are made at about 40 or less yards. In the case of ducks, the hunter should be able to distinguish body colors clearly for the bird to be in range. For geese, particularly Canadas, the birds should look like a flight of jet bombers at tree top level. Learn the characteristics of the waterfowl you plan to hunt and check the experts to be sure you know how to tell when they are in range. "Skybusting" results in cripples and spoils the sport for everyone.

The Choice of Guns

The choice of guns for waterfowl hunting is just as open to argument as it is for upland game. The selection of action styles, as we have indicated, is largely a matter of personal preference. All of them are capable of doing a good job. Waterfowl, however, are generally larger than most upland species. They are also usually hunted at longer ranges. Thus a 12 gauge, full choke with long range loads is the most popular style. Full choke 16 or 20 gauge guns, particularly with magnum loads, are also popular.

For decoying birds, a modified choke is often sufficient,

although not necessary. As is the case with all types of shotgun shooting, experience is, in the last analysis, the best guide.

Waterfowl Etiquette

The rules of basic good sportsmanship are again the guide to etiquette in a duck or goose blind. A number of these points have already been covered: don't be a "skybuster" and do hunt with a dog, for example. If two or more hunters are in a blind together, assign areas for shooting. If, by chance, both of you shoot at the same bird, remember the golden rule! If you have filled your limit and your partner is having his troubles, don't shoot his birds for him. In the first place, it is against the law and in the second, it is poor sportsmanship. Observe the rules of safe gun handling to the letter both for your own safety and that of your companions.

CHAPTER 10

Big Game with a Shotgun

The shotgun is designed for use in hunting birds and small animals and it is ideally suited for this purpose. However, it is a versatile firearm and, as such, has application for other purposes. In some of the more heavily populated areas of this country, there are laws requiring its use, with rifled slugs or buckshot, for hunting deer or comparable sized animals. In most cases, because these projectiles have much shorter effective ranges than center-fire rifle cartridges, this theory has some validity. A comparison of down range ballistics, for both types of ammunition, bears this out.

While some hunters may argue with this thesis, based on the fact that a well-trained rifleman uses his firearm safely within the limits of the terrain he hunts—whether he is in the wilds of Wyoming or a relatively populated area—the fact remains that such regulations do exist. Recognizing this, it then becomes important for hunters to know just how effective rifled slugs and buckshot are and what can be expected of them in the hunting field.

Actually, at ranges of less than 75 yards, rifled slugs are very effective from the standpoint of remaining velocity, energy, and accuracy. At 40 or less yards, buckshot is also capable of killing deer, though it is not as dependable at longer ranges.

Tests fired by ammunition manufacturers and independent researchers indicate that, with rifled slugs, five shot groups of from 3 to 5 inches extreme spread can be expected at 50 yards. While groups of this size are hardly going to put anyone "in the money" in an accuracy tournament, they are obviously adequate for downing large game at relatively short ranges. Further tests have indicated that best results with rifled slugs and buckshot are obtained with cylinder bore barrels although, occasionally, modified barrels will give satisfactory groups. It comes down to the business of test firing the ammunition in individual guns to determine the best performance. Before getting deeper into this subject, definitions of rifled slugs and buckshot seem in order.

Characteristics of Rifled Slugs

A rifled slug is a projectile made from soft lead with a hollow base and solid nose. The hollow base is expanded, by the force of the burning powder gases, to fill the bore of the shotgun when the slug is fired. Spiral grooves are swaged into its outside to impart a spin on firing. In effect, the rifled slug is the latter-day descendant of the round ball fired in old smooth-bore muskets, used by hunters and the military before the perfection of rifling cut into barrels. The swaged spiral grooves have added a new dimension, however, by giving the necessary stability in flight. A slug does not spin very rapidly but its spiral motion is sufficient for the purpose.

A 12 gauge slug weighs 1 ounce; a 16 gauge, ⅞ of an ounce; a 20 gauge, ⅝ of an ounce; and a .410 gauge, 1/5 of an ounce. No slugs are made in 28 gauge.

In terms of grain weight, the frame of reference usually used to describe rifle bullets, rifled slugs measure up as follows:

12 gauge	—	415 grains
16 gauge	—	350 grains
20 gauge	—	282 grains
410 gauge	—	93 grains

By comparison, the heaviest bullet weight offered in the .30-06 caliber rifle cartridge, one of the most popular deer loads, weighs 220 grains. The only rifle calibers available with heavier bullets are designed for use against large game such as elephants—the .458 Winchester, for example, which has a 510 grain bullet in its largest size.

Caliber comparisons are also revealing. The bore of a 12 gauge shotgun is equivalent to .73 caliber, the 16 gauge to .67 caliber, the 20 to .60 caliber, and the .410, of course, to .410 caliber. Comparisons, again, with popular deer rifles, most of which are .30 caliber or less, show that even the smallest gauges of rifled slugs are loaded with quite a chunk of lead!

Rifled Slug Ballistics

The ultimate criterion in killing power for a cartridge, be it a rifled slug shot shell or a center fire load, is a combination of remaining velocity and remaining energy at average hunting ranges.

Obviously a comparison of down-range ballistics, at extreme ranges, between some of the newer, flat-shooting, high-velocity cartridges and rifled slugs wouldn't demonstrate much beyond the readily apparent fact that smoothbores aren't designed for long range work. However, a comparison between some of the popular, low velocity "brush" calibers and slugs is revealing. The table on the next page, which was worked out by the Ballistics Department of Remington Arms, is illustrative.

From this tabulation, it is apparent that a 12 gauge rifled slug, at 50 yards, delivers far more energy than the .30 carbine cartridge, even though it is traveling at lower velocity. The .30 carbine, in spite of its increased popularity due to the number of surplus military rifles available, is perhaps a poor example. Most experts have long agreed that, ballistically, this cartridge is a pretty poor performer.

However, even in comparison with so-called "brush" cartridges such as the .30-30, .30 Remington, .35 Remington and

Gauge or Caliber	Projectile Weight	Velocity in Feet per second at Muzzle	25 yds.	50 yds.	75 yds.	100 yds.	Energy in Foot pounds at Muzzle	25 yds.	50 yds.	75 yds.	100 yds.	Drop in inches at 25 yds.	50 yds.	75 yds.	100 yds.	Mid Range Trajectory in inches for Range of 25 yds.	50 yds.	75 yds.	100 yds.
12 ga.	1 oz.	1600	1365	1175	1040	950	2485	1810	1340	1050	875	.5	2.1	5.3	10.4	.1	.6	1.5	3.1
16 ga.	7/8 oz.	1600	1365	1175	1040	950	2175	1585	1175	920	765	.5	2.1	5.3	10.4	.1	.6	1.5	3.1
20 ga.	5/8 oz.	1600	1365	1175	1040	950	1555	1130	840	655	550	.5	2.1	5.3	10.4	.1	.6	1.5	3.1
410 ga.	1/5 oz.	1830	1560	1335	1150	1025	650	475	345	255	205	.4	1.6	4.1	8.2	.1	.4	1.2	2.5
30-30 Win.	170 gr	2220	2130	2050	1970	1890	1860	1710	1590	1460	1350	.2	.9	2.1	3.9	.05	.2	.6	1.0
30 Rem.	170 gr	2120	2040	1970	1890	1820	1700	1570	1460	1350	1250	.2	.9	2.4	4.3	.05	.2	.6	1.2
30 Carbine	110 gr	1980	1860	1750	1640	1540	955	845	750	655	580	.3	1.2	2.8	5.3	.08	.3	.7	1.5
35 Rem.	200 gr	2100	2000	1900	1800	1710	1960	1780	1600	1440	1300	.2	1.0	2.5	4.5	.05	.3	.6	1.3
44 Rem. Mag.	240 gr	1750	1640	1540	1450	1360	1630	1430	1260	1120	985	.4	1.6	3.5	6.8	.1	.4	.9	1.8

.44 Remington Magnum, the 12 gauge slug doesn't measure up too badly. It doesn't have the velocity or energy of any of these loads, but it certainly is perfectly capable of killing a deer, or comparable size animal, with no difficulty, at short range. Even at 100 yards it has enough knockdown power to do the job.

The smaller gauges, as might well be expected, do not perform as well. However, at short ranges, they are adequate, although the .410 gauge is marginal.

Shotguns for Rifled Slugs

In recognition of the growing popularity of these loads for use on game, most shotgun manufacturers now offer special models with open cylinder bores and rifle sights. These smooth bores make the problem of aiming a shotgun far simpler than would be the case with a standard scattergun tube.

As is the case with any rifle, however, it behooves owners of shotguns to be used in firing rifled slugs, whether they are equipped with rifle sights or not, to sight in their guns before going afield. This, in the last analysis, is the only way a shooter can know definitely what type of groups he can expect and where to hold on game animals.

It is also true that single-barreled guns are far better than doubles—particularly those of the side-by-side persuasion. The best side-by-sides tend to crossfire with slugs, because these guns are designed to deliver full patterns of shot, not slugs, at a center of impact 40 yards from the muzzle. Over-and-under doubles, however, do not present the same problems.

Typical 12 gauge deer gun

Buckshot Loads

As has been indicated, buckshot loads do not have quite the range of rifled slugs. Far larger than the biggest standard shot size—BB's which are each .18 inches in diameter—buckshot loads range from number 4 (.24 inches in diameter) to 00 (.33 inches in diameter). The intermediate sizes are 3 (.25 inches in diameter) and 0 (.32 inches in diameter). The number of buckshot in a given shell ranges from 9 or 12 in a 12 gauge 00 buck to 41 in a 12 gauge 3 inch magnum shell loaded with 4 buck. Loads are offered in 12, 16 and 20 gauges. Dispersion of the pellets at 40 yards is apt to be pretty wide with any size of buckshot. However, several pellets can be counted on to hit the mark. Because the size of each rivals many rifle bullets (the .32 caliber of 0 buck for example) and their penetrating power at less than 40 yards is pretty good, they can be used successfully on deer at short ranges. Buckshot is not generally as effective as rifled slugs, however.

From all of this, the hunter is safe in drawing the conclusion that rifled slugs and buckshot, particularly in 12 gauge, are more than adequate for most medium-sized game. In the last analysis, as is the case in almost any shooting situation, the secret of success with these loads, and shotguns designed to fire them, is in the ability of the user. With all the skills of today's firearms and ammunition designers and manufacturers, most gun and ammunition combinations are capable of delivering results far in excess of the abilities of the average shooter.

CHAPTER 11

Safety Rules and Shotgun Care

Statistically speaking, shooting in general, and shotgun shooting in particular, is an extremely safe sport. It is true that, during every hunting season, stories of accidents appear in the news. An analysis of these stories over the years shows, however, that the death rate resulting from firearms accidents, per 100,000 of population, has decreased by 25 percent in the last decade. Insurance company statistics show that football, a sport with only a very small number of participants, accounts for many more accidents than does shooting.

Impressive though this record may be, even one accident—no matter what the cause—can spell tragedy for the victim and his family. It, therefore, is incumbent upon every shooter to obey the rules of safe gun handling to the letter.

The Basic Safety Rules

Earlier discussions of etiquette in the hunting field have covered a number of the principles of safe gun handling. The importance of this subject justifies their repetition here, however. For many years, the sporting arms and ammunition industry has distributed a small leaflet to hunters listing "The Ten Commandments of Safety." These rules are:

1. Treat every gun with the respect due a loaded gun. This is the cardinal rule of gun safety.
2. Watch that muzzle! Carry your gun safely; keep the safety on until you are ready to shoot.

3. Unload guns when not in use. Take down or have actions open. Guns should be carried in cases to shooting areas.
4. Be sure barrel is clear of obstructions, and that you have ammunition only of the proper size for the guns that you carry.
5. Be sure of your target before you pull the trigger; know identifying features of the game you hunt.
6. Never point a gun at anything you do not want to shoot; avoid all horseplay.
7. Never climb a tree or fence or jump a ditch with a loaded gun; never pull a gun toward you by the muzzle.
8. Never shoot a bullet at a flat, hard surface or water; at target practice, be sure your backstop is adequate.
9. Store guns and ammunition separately, beyond reach of children.
10. Avoid alcoholic beverages before or during shooting.

These are good sound rules, based on practical experience in the hunting field. Knowing the rules alone is not enough, however. Their proper application comes through practicing them in the hunting field or on trap and skeet fields.

Hunter Safety Training

Some years ago, the National Rifle Association of America inaugurated a hunter safety-training program. A number of states now have laws making it mandatory for new shooters to pass this course before they can obtain a hunting license. In other areas, voluntary hunter safety programs are conducted in schools or by sportsmen's groups under NRA auspices. This is a good plan and experts are agreed that it has played a vital part in keeping firearms accidents to a minimum. Indications are that more and more states will make this program compulsory in the future.

Know Your Gun

One of the cardinal rules of safety, not mentioned in the above tabulation, is to know your gun. Before you do anything else, when you acquire a new firearm, find out how to load and unload it. Learn how to operate the safety and use it at all times. Learn the gun's capacity and its operating characteristics. Don't pick up a friend's gun, to examine it, unless you know how it works. If you don't know, find out. Above all, remember to open the action and check to see if the gun is loaded before doing anything else. Don't just check the chamber, look in the magazine too. One of the most frequent refrains, heard after an accident, is "I didn't know it was loaded." There is no excuse for this kind of ignorance.

The rule about checking the barrel for obstructions is also worth more emphasis. Occasionally a hunter will stumble, when afield, jamming the muzzle of his gun into mud or snow. If these obstructions are not cleared, they can cause a barrel to burst, with often serious results.

The problem of loading 20 gauge shells, into a 12 gauge gun, is also dangerous. Now and then, when a hunter has been afield with his 20, he will leave a few shells in his hunting coat pocket. He will then go out with his 12 and, inadvertently, put a 20 gauge shell into the chamber. The smaller shell will slip down into the barrel out of sight. The unwary hunter may forget it and slip a 12 in the chamber behind it. The result is usually a blown barrel and an injury.

General Care

A sporting shotgun is basically a mechanical device. Its parts are made of metal and they are subject to rusting and wear as are all comparable products. In the early days of center-fire, primed, black-powder shells, barrel rusting was a considerable problem. Shotguns required cleaning after every use because black powder was corrosive as were the mercuric priming mixtures used. The introduction of smokeless powders, which do not cause rusting, solved part of the problem. In the mid-1920's, Remington Arms Company, Inc., introduced their "Kleanbore" priming mixture which was also non-corrosive. Other ammunition companies followed and, as a result, it is no longer necessary to clean guns after each firing.

This does not mean, however, that you can just shoot them and hang them up. In gas-operated guns, in particular, residue of unburned powder can build up in the venting hole, the piston area, and the chamber. Periodic cleaning is necessary to alleviate this problem. In addition, if you plan to put your gun away for any period of time, it should be cleaned and oiled to prevent rusting.

Problems of barrel rusting or the lack of it not withstanding, shotguns do need periodic maintenance to keep them in good shape. Properly cared for, the average scattergun can last a lifetime. Over-oiling can be just as much a problem, however, as lack of sufficient care. Too much lubricant can rot the wood of the stock and fore-end. In addition, excess oil tends to gum up the chamber or action causing extraction and functioning problems.

Cleaning Procedures

The basic tools for cleaning and maintaining a shotgun are not very complex. You should have a jointed wooden cleaning rod with brass brushes and felt balls for each gauge. In addition, you will need a can of lubricating oil, a tube of graphite (mixed with oil), a can of powder solvent, patches of cotton or other soft cloth, and some rust preventive grease or oil.

The first step, in cleaning the bore of a shotgun, is to run an oil-soaked patch through it. This can be followed with another oiled patch if necessary. Do not leave too much oil in the barrel, however. If there is an accumulation of lead residue just forward of the chamber, or powder residue in the chamber, use a brass bristle brush to remove these deposits.

In the case of automatics or pumps, the trigger assembly and the block should be removed periodically. Soaking in a powder solvent should remove powder residue and other dirt. The parts should then be dried off and reassembled. The pistons of gas-operated automatics should be disassembled periodically and thoroughly cleaned. Check the vent holes in the barrel, also, to be sure they are not clogged with powder residue.

Manufacturers' instruction folders, which are furnished with every new shotgun, contain detailed information on maintenance. Follow them carefully and you will preserve the life of your firearm.

Gun Storage

Gun cases are designed for carrying, not storing guns. When you return from a trip afield take your gun out of the case, and put it in a rack. Stored in the case, it may sweat and rust.

Perspiration, or "sweat," is a particular enemy of firearms.

After a gun has been handled, the metal parts should be wiped lightly with oil. If they are not, fingerprints are apt to be preserved for posterity in rust. If you take a gun out of the cold into a warm room, it is apt to sweat, causing rust.

If you plan to use your shotgun in cold weather, remove all the oil and coat the working parts with powdered graphite. If you don't do this, you're in for some frustrating malfunctions.

The force of recoil and the normal vibrations of firing can cause some parts of a firearm to work loose. Check these parts from time to time and tighten them up if necessary.

With the advent of smokeless powder and non-corrosive primers, gun care is no longer a great problem. Observing the few simple guide lines outlined above, however, will help to preserve the life of your scattergun and give you many more years of enjoyment with it.

CHAPTER 12

Roll Your Own

There is nothing new about reloading shotgun shells. In the early days of center-fire, breech-loading shotguns, as we have already seen, shells were always purchased primed and empty and then loaded and reloaded several times. The introduction of the first loaded factory shells in this country, by the Union Metallic Cartridge Company, was quite an event. However, hand loading continued up until the introduction and perfection of smokeless powders. These new propellants required more technical skill to handle than was the case with black powder. As a result, the practice of hand loading, and reloading of shotgun shells, gradually died down.

The Renaissance of Reloading

The post World War II years, in America, were witness to a great surge of interest in "do it yourself" activities. The perfection of easy-to-handle power tools, the great boom in suburban living, and a resurgence of the notion that American males were "jacks-of-all-trades," were all contributing factors. The shooting sports were not neglected in the development of this phenomenon. Clay target enthusiasts in particular, because they do a lot more shooting than the average hunter, found that it was fun and economical to "roll their own" shotgun shells. As a result, the business of manufacturing and selling reloading equipment underwent a rebirth and a tremendous growth.

A number of far-sighted entrepreneurs saw the possibilities

of the trend and set about designing easy-to-use and reasonably priced tools for the job, and they did a good job of promoting the latent interest. At first, there was some apprehension, on the part of ammunition manufacturers, that reloading would have an adverse effect on the sale of loaded rounds. Experience soon showed, however, that the reverse was true. There is a limit to the number of times a shell can be reloaded, which means new shells must be purchased periodically. In addition, reloaders tend to shoot a great deal more, after taking up the hobby, than they did before. They must also buy components including shot, wads, powder, primers and cases; all of which are made by the industry. The long range result has been an increase in interest in shooting and more sales of loaded rounds and components.

Quality of Reloads

In some registered shoots—those conducted under the auspices of either the National Skeet Shooting Association or the Amateur Trapshooting Association—the use of reloads is prohibited. The reason for this has nothing to do with the quality of "home-brewed" ammunition. Instead it is designed to insure that only loads of the maximum power allowed under the rules are used. Actually, with the equipment now available, it is possible to reload shells of very good quality.

With the advent of plastic shell cases, which as we have seen, are now being made by all of the major ammunition companies, it is possible to reload a given case as many as 10 or 15 times.

The Steps in Reloading

The basic construction of a modern target load shotgun shell is shown in the picture on page 121. All of the components shown are obviously needed to produce handloads.

Components of the modern target load shotgun shell

The first step is the choice of a reloading tool. The equipment available ranges from relatively inexpensive and simple hand-operated devices to rather complex, expensive, motor driven machines which are actually miniatures of the equipment used in ammunition factories. The differences in the products turned out by this variety of tools are slight. All of them are capable of making serviceable ammunition. The bigger and fancier machines are more automated and can thus be operated more rapidly for volume production.

The simplest type of tool, which is reliable enough to produce serviceable hand loads, consists of a small bench press and a set of simple dies. The first step, in using one of these machines, is knocking out the fired primer and inserting a new one. This process is known as decapping and recapping. The shell is placed under the decapping position on the press and the handle is pulled down. Some pressure is required to remove the old primer. If it comes out too easily, throw the shell away as the new primer would probably be loose if inserted.

A new primer is then placed in a holder on the base of the tool. The shell is positioned, head first, over this holder and the handle is again pulled down. A rammer presses the shell head home over the primer inserting it to the proper depth.

The third step consists of pressing the shell into a die designed to bring it back as close as possible to its original diameter. This is known as resizing and it is particularly important. Some expansion is bound to take place when a shell is fired and without resizing, the reload may not fit in the chamber of the gun.

In the simplest tools, powder is then poured in with a hand dipper. In more complex machines, there is a container for powder (and another for shot) mounted on the frame. A device in the bottom of the powder container, which can be adjusted or changed for different loads, then measures out the correct amount of powder and lets it fall into place in the shell.

Particular care should be taken, whether a hand dipper or an automatic charger is used, to insure that it measures only the correct grain weight of powder for the load desired and *not* dram weight. As you will recall from earlier discussions, dram equivalent measurements shown on factory loaded shotshell boxes are a carryover from black powder days. They have no relevance to the actual charge of powder used and are only intended as an indication of the velocity of the load.

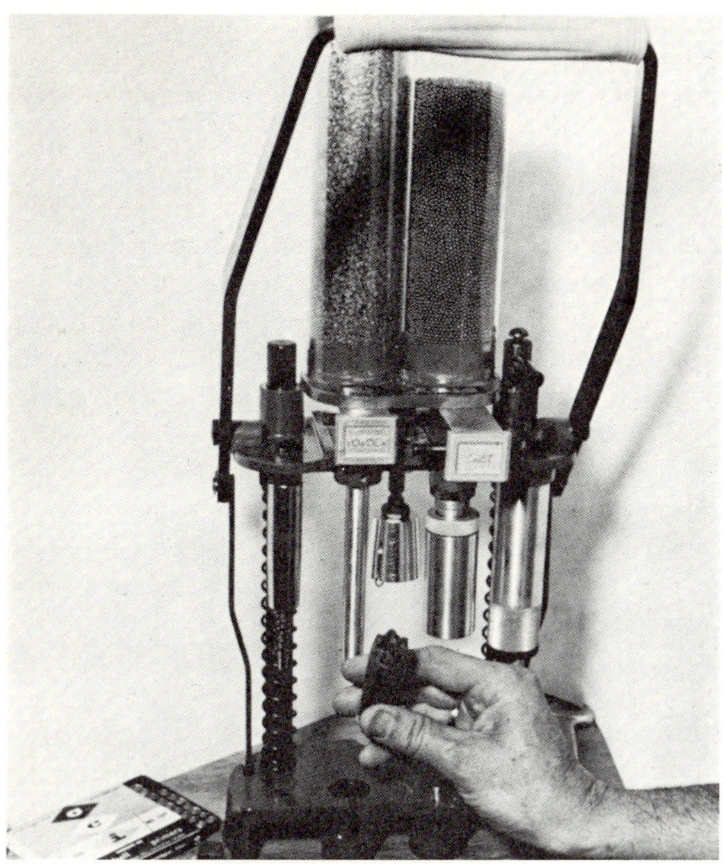

A typical reloading tool shows the shot shell after the E-zy Crimp Starter has been used to fold the case preparatory to the final sizing and crimping.

Loading this amount of smokeless powder could be very dangerous. DuPont bulk smokeless powders are the only exception to this rule.

The wad or wads are then placed in the shell mouth. Seating is accomplished by means of a rammer. It is important for good shell performance to use the correct amount of pressure in seating the wad, or wads. This varies from 30 to 100 pounds depending on the type of powder and wads being used. Most tools have a graduated gauge for measuring wad-seating pressure.

The shell is then moved to a position under the shot charger (or a hand dipper designed to hold the correct amount of shot). The shot is placed over the wads.

Crimping is the next step. A special die is used which folds the mouth into the pie-shaped crimp used in modern shells. In the case of plastic shells a starter crimp, to insure a good fold, is necessary. In some tools, the resizing operation takes place after final loading while in others it occurs after priming.

The final shell is inspected visually and then placed in a box ready for use.

Detailed description of the operation of the large variety of tools on the market today is beyond the scope of this book. Whatever tool you use, make sure you know how it works and follow the instructions furnished with it in detail.

Hints on Components

No reload can be any better than the basic ingredients that go into it. The first consideration, obviously, is the fired cases used. Inspect them carefully before you start. Segregate shells of different brands. Base-wad height variations, and other differences in design characteristics, make this necessary. Check the cases for any evidence of pin holes or indications that the head has worked loose. Make sure the base wads are firmly in place. If the mouth looks thin or worn, discard the shell—it has done its duty.

There are a number of good powders on the market. Whatever brand you use, be sure you check the grain weight the manufacturer specifies. Reloading tool manuals and powder-makers' literature will give you this data.

As we have seen, one piece plastic wad columns and shot containers have pretty well replaced the old felt and cardboard combinations, particularly in target loads. The new systems are also much simpler to load. One operation does the whole job.

Primers are made by all of the major ammunition companies and several other concerns as well. Just be sure you get the right size for the type of shell you are using. Shot, made by the major companies, is also readily available in a full range of sizes.

Plastic shell bodies are the greatest recent boon to reloaders. The old paper shells could be reused no more than four or five times while there are recorded examples of ten to fifteen loadings with the plastics. The only problem with them is the need to use a special starter die to insure good crimping.

Economics of Reloading

One of the prime reasons people reload shotgun shells, aside from the hobby aspect, is cost. Estimates of the savings over factory loads vary because prices of components change—lead for shot in particular. Of course reloaders don't calculate the cost of the labor required, as factories must. On the basis of out-of-pocket expense, however, reloads cost about half the price of new target loads.

Safety

During the early days of the resurgence of interest in "roll your own" shot shells, there was concern on the part of some people about the safety of these loads. Reloading tools are as foolproof as the manufacturers can make them and, if instructions are followed carefully, there is no great danger. The human element must be considered, however, and people are sometimes careless, or they try to experiment with new loads without sufficient knowledge. Obviously this can cause trouble. Fortunately, however, the incidence of accidents with hand loaded shotgun shells is remarkably low.

A neat work area is important for reloading. Powder and primers should be handled carefully and stowed under lock and key, out of the reach of children. In the small quantities required by the average reloader, and in the containers in which it is sold, powder is perfectly safe if properly stored. The same is true of primers.

Reloading Hunting Shells

The greatest interest in reloading shotshells, as was indicated earlier, has been on the part of trap and skeet shooters who consume large quantities of ammunition. The average hunter, who only uses two or three boxes of shells in a season anyway, seldom bothers with it. He could hardly justify the investment in equipment involved and there is little reason for him to reload anyway. Some target shooters who are also hunters do reload, however, and sometimes, groups of hunters band together to set up a reloading operation.

The same basic equipment, with minor adjustments, can be used for hunting loads.

For the hobbyist, be he target shooter or hunter, reloading can be a fascinating, and money saving, pastime. Its growth has spawned a whole new industry designed to cater to its demands. Factory loaded ammunition is still of better quality, however, and new developments in the future may well widen this gap.

CHAPTER 13

The Future of the Shooting Sports

The sports of hunting and shooting, which have a tradition as old as time, are facing serious problems in America today. The difficulties come from two sources: the encroachment of civilization and the consequent destruction of large areas of the natural habitat of wildlife; and the opposition of sometimes well meaning, but often misinformed, people to hunting and shooting. Of these two, the first presents the greatest potential long range threat.

Background to Modern Conservation

In the days when the first settlers arrived on this continent, there was an abundance of game. The notion of conserving this great natural resource never occurred to our forebears. Wildlife was a source of food and they relied on it to provide meat for the table. The development of cattle ranching and poultry farming was a long way in the future.

Population growth changed this situation, however. As the number of people grew, the demands on available land increased also. The decline of the American bison (buffalo) and the whooping crane, and the demise of the passenger pigeon, have often been blamed on hunters.

In the case of the buffalo and the passenger pigeon, there is no question that hunting was a partial factor. However, the march of civilization, which destroyed the habitat of these creatures, was a far greater villain. Buffalo were creatures of the open range. They required vast areas to maintain themselves. The building of railroads and the extension of fenced-in grazing lands were the greatest factors in their partial elimination. Buffalo competed, for grazing land, with domestic cattle, and they were slaughtered at least partly because of this competition. In addition, their living habits, in vast numbers, were not compatible with fenced-in agriculture. Today, on a limited scale in protected areas, they are undergoing a renaissance, but the demands of domestic cattle raising preclude a return to the vast herds of a century ago. There just isn't room enough for them.

Whooping cranes, shy and retiring birds without any great facility for adapting to changing conditions, were never very large in numbers. The inexorable march of agricultural progress, which encroached on their natural habitat, has been the biggest factor in their decline. In essence, their present condition is a modern counterpart of the theory of the survival of the fittest. Noble efforts in their behalf may insure that small numbers survive but any great increase in the whooping crane population is doubtful, no matter what we may do to perpetuate the species.

The problems of the passenger pigeon are comparable to those of the buffalo. As has been indicated their extinction was hastened by advancing civilization. It is true that they were slaughtered in vast numbers but destruction of their habitat by man was equally important.

Wildlife Today

The problems of wildlife today have some parallel to the situations described above. It is true that our approach towards conservation is vastly different from that of our ancestors. We recognize that game is not an unlimited resource and that civilization, not the hunter, is its greatest enemy. The pro-

Canadas over Remington Farms, Chestertown, Maryland

posed Rampart Dam in Alaska is a case in point. If this project is approved, it will cause the flooding of millions of acres of some of the finest waterfowl nesting areas of the Pacific flyway. In addition, it will destroy an important spawning area for salmon and the habitat of untold numbers of large and small game animals and birds. This desecration of nature is being proposed in the name of inexpensive hydroelectric power, in an area that has little demonstrated need for more electricity on such a scale. In theory, transmission lines would carry some of this hydroelectric power to Washington and Oregon but at a cost hardly competitive in price.

There are similar schemes afoot in many areas of the country. In Chapter 9 we reviewed the problem of encroaching agricultural projects in relation to waterfowl populations and we discussed some of the things being done about these problems. There are other encouraging signs. Conservation groups are fighting against projects such as the Rampart Dam. Obviously, a balance must be struck between the needs of our ever growing population and the desire to preserve some segments of our wilderness areas for posterity.

Conservation Funds

Millions of dollars every year are contributed to this cause by hunters. An excise tax is levied on the sale of sporting firearms and ammunition. All of this money is apportioned to the various states on a matching basis, to be used exclusively for wildlife management purposes. Fees from the sale of hunting licenses, fees from the sale of Federal duck stamps, and large sums contributed by private groups such as the Isaac Walton League, The National Wildlife Federation, The Wildlife Management Institute, Ducks Unlimited, and others go for similar purposes.

Two recently enacted Federal laws are also bound to help. The first is the Land and Water Conservation Act which will potentially make available up to $180 million a year for outdoor recreation planning, land purchase and development. The second is the National Wilderness Preservation System Act which will conserve up to 23½ million acres of national forests for recreational purposes, including hunting and fishing.

All of these programs are encouraging steps towards mainte-

A. L. Nelson, Director, Patuxent Research Refuge in stand of millet, an excellent duck food

nance and preservation of our wildlife resources. Regulation of bag limits and seasons are set by trained game management experts in the various states and the Federal Government. As a result game supplies are at an all time high and game crops harvested every year are controlled so that only birds and animals that might otherwise fall prey to natural predators are actually taken. A good case can be made for the fact that, thanks to all this interest, hunted species are probably better off than non-hunted birds and animals.

With greater demands upon agricultural land, caused at least in part by the seemingly never-ending spread of urban areas into former farm land, it has become increasingly apparent that wildlife, particularly upland game and waterfowl, is a by-product of farming. Much of the effort of private and public organizations in the field today is devoted to developing programs for farmers which show that sound land use is compatible with the needs of both agriculture and the preservation of wildlife.

The battle is far from won, however, and the long range threats are very real. Every drained prairie pothole, many new public roads and dams, and numerous new shopping centers and housing developments are threats to our wildlife populations. It is up to our public agencies, inspired by the interests of sportsmen and other lovers of wildlife and the out-of-doors, to weigh each new project very carefully. A sound balance can and must be struck between the needs of our growing population and the preservation of our wildlife heritage.

Legislative Problems

In Chapter 1, we tried to outline some of the joys and thrills that hunting can provide. In this chapter, we have reviewed the conservation contributions of hunters. For some people, however, the pleasures that hunting affords to its millions of devotees are alien at best. For various reasons, they have scruples against the killing of game. There are probably no arguments that would change these people's minds. Their opposition, to so-called blood sports, is seldom shaken when it is pointed out to them that man is a carnivorous creature. They have difficulty working up the same sympathy for a hog, steer, or lamb, in the slaughtering pen, that they profess for the deer or antelope on the range. The fact that wild creatures have a chance of survival, while domestic meat animals have none, interests them very little. They can eat farm-raised turkey, duck or chicken with great relish while shedding tears of mourning for the poor white wing dove. Logic, in these

Multiflora rose hedges make excellent cover for rabbits, quail and many song birds at Remington Farms

cases, is not their forte. Their is little use in arguing with them, provided they do not try to impose their scruples on others.

Other well-meaning people would vastly restrict the rights of law abiding citizens to own and use sporting firearms in the hope that, by so doing, crimes with firearms would be reduced. These people's motives are laudable, although their logic is sometimes suspect. Among the most frequently proposed firearms control measures, are laws requiring registration and/or licensing. The fact that criminals could hardly be expected to obey these laws is of apparent small consequence to their proponents.

There is no question that it is within the proper province of legislative bodies, be they local, state or national, to enact regulations designed to keep firearms out of the hands of criminals, juvenile delinquents, and other undesirables. Care must be taken, however, to insure that such laws do not unduly restrict the rights of the vast majority of law abiding gun owners. Legislation which makes stiff punishments mandatory, for the use of guns in the commission of crimes, certainly meets this test. Laws which legislate against the ownership of firearms are suspect.

In the final analysis, a gun itself is an inanimate object hardly capable of doing either right or wrong. The demented mind of a criminal, intent on robbery or murder, is hardly apt to be deterred by the choice of weapons. If a gun isn't available, he will use a knife, a blunt instrument or whatever else he can find. The ultimate solution to the problems of crime and violence would seem to lie in solving the deep sociological and educational difficulties that contribute to the *breeding of slums,* not banning guns.

In spite of the conservation and legislative problems facing the sports of hunting and shooting, there is great promise for the future. Our ever-growing economy is contributing to a great increase in interest in all forms of outdoor recreation. People have more money to spend and more leisure time in which to spend it than ever before in our history. Participant sports such as hunting, shooting and fishing are reaping the reward of this prosperity. With the intelligent interest of all concerned, we can insure that these activities will endure.

Glossary

ACTION A part of the breech mechanism of a firearm. Specifically, that part which holds the cartridge or shell in the locked position. Typical shotgun actions are: autoloader, pump, break-open, lever and bolt.

ACTION BARS Connecting rods between the fore-end of a pump gun and the breech block, or the gas cylinder of an autoloader and the breech block.

ACTION PORT An opening in the side of the action of a pump, autoloading or lever action firearm through which single rounds are loaded and fired shells are ejected.

ALL-BORE A term used in skeet-shooting to describe events open to guns of 12 gauge or smaller size.

AUTOLOADER A firearm in which the force of recoil or expanding gases is used to eject the fired round and feed a new round into the chamber ready for firing. A distinct trigger pull is needed for each shot.

AUTOMATIC A firearm that operates continously as long as the trigger is depressed; a machine gun. Autoloading (or semi-automatic) rifles and shotguns, which require a distinct pull of the trigger for each shot, are sometimes mistakenly called automatics.

AXIS OF THE BORE A straight line projected down the exact center of the bore of a firearm.

BALLISTICS The science of projectile motion. Interior ballistics deals with motion of projectiles within the barrel of a firearm. Exterior ballistics is concerned with the flight of projectiles after they leave the muzzle.

BARREL The metal tube through which a bullet or shot charge passes before leaving the muzzle of a firearm.

BASE WAD Filler material inserted in the head of a shotgun shell ahead of the powder charge.

BLACK POWDER A propellant mixture composed of saltpeter, charcoal and sulphur.

BLOCK That part of a firearm which holds the shell or cartridge firmly in the chamber when the action is closed.

BOLT ACTION A type of action in which a steel rod, similar to a door bolt, is used to lock the cartridge or shell in the chamber.

BORE A hole in the center of the barrel of a firearm.

BREECH The portion of the barrel into which the shell or cartridge is inserted. The rear end of a barrel.

BREECH-LOADING A gun which loads through the breech.

BUCK SHOT A large size of shot.

BULLET A single projectile fired from a rifle.

CALIBER The diameter of the bore of a rifle measured in hundredths or thousandths of an inch or in millimeters.

CARTRIDGE A metallic case which contains a primer, a propellant charge and a bullet or projectile.

CENTER-FIRE CARTRIDGE A cartridge which has a primer located in the center of the base of its head.

CHAMBER The enlarged portion of the barrel of a firearm (at the breech end) in which a cartridge or shell is placed for firing.

CHOKE A constriction of the bore of a shotgun, at the muzzle end, designed to control the shot pattern.

CLAY TARGET A circular disc of clay and pitch used as a target for trap or skeet shooting. Also known as a clay pigeon.

COMPONENTS The parts of a shotgun shell including case, primer, wads, powder and shot.

CRIMP The forward portion of a shotshell case which is folded in to form a closure to hold the shot in place.

DAMASCUS BARREL A barrel manufactured by twisting red hot strips of iron and steel around a mandrel. Not safe to shoot with modern ammunition.

DOUBLE A shotgun with two barrels; located either side-by-side or one-over-the-other.

DOUBLES Two clay targets thrown simultaneously in either trap or skeet shooting.

EJECTOR The device used to throw a fired shell or cartridge from a gun.

FIELD GUN A shotgun used for hunting in the field as opposed to clay target shooting.

FIELD LOAD A shotgun shell used for upland game hunting of small game or birds at relatively short ranges.

FIRING PIN The device which strikes the primer of a shell or cartridge to ignite it.

FORE-END The forward part of a firearm stock used as a hand support under the barrel.

FOWLING PIECE A colloquial term used to describe a shotgun used for bird hunting.

GAS-OPERATED A firearm which uses part of the force of the gas, created by exploding powder, to operate the action.

GAUGE The system of measurement used to describe the diameter of the bore of a shotgun.

GUNPOWDER The propellant charge used in firearms. Black powder was the earliest type. Smokeless powder is used today.

HAMMER The part of the action that actuates the firing pin of a firearm.

HAND GUN A small concealable firearm which can be held in one hand.

HAND TRAP A hand-held spring-actuated device for throwing clay targets.

HIGH BASE A shotgun shell on which the metal head extends fairly high up on the paper or plastic body. Used for long-range shooting.

HIGH HOUSE One of the two structures on a skeet field which house the traps.

LEVER ACTION An action operated by a lever which is part of the trigger guard.

LOCK The firing mechanism for a muzzle-loading firearm.

LOCKING LUGS A series of projections on the forward end of a bolt used to lock it into the chamber of a firearm.

LOW BASE A shotgun shell on which the metal base does not extend very high on the paper or metal tube. Used for small upland game.

LOW HOUSE One of the two structures on a skeet field which house the traps.

MAGAZINE The device on a repeating firearm used to hold extra ammunition.

MAGNUM An extra high powered shotgun shell for long-range use. A shotgun designed for firing magnum shells.

MARK The call used by a skeet shooter to request the throwing of a bird from the low house.

METALLIC CARTRIDGE A self-contained cartridge with a metal case.

MUSKET A smooth bore firearm of early vintage.

MUZZLE The forward end of a gun barrel.

MUZZLE LOADING A firearm that is loaded through the muzzle.

NON-CORROSIVE PRIMING A priming mixture, used in modern ammunition, which does not cause barrel rusting.

OVER-AND-UNDER A double-barreled firearm with one barrel located on top of the other.

PATTERN The distribution of a shotgun shell charge in the target area.

PISTOL A hand-held firearm.

PRIME The process of preparing a muzzle-loading gun for firing.

PRIMER The device used to ignite the powder charge.

PROJECTILE A missile propelled by a firearm; a bullet.

PROPELLANT The explosive mixture used to propel projectile or shot charge. Gunpowder.

PULL The word used to call for a target in trap or skeet shooting.

PUMP ACTION An action style in which the bolt is opened by pulling back on the fore-end. Also known as a slide action.

RECOIL The rearward thrust of a gun caused by the expansion of burning powder gases used to propel the projectile.

RELOADING The process of reusing once-fired shells by removing the old primer and inserting new primer, powder, wads and shot.

REPEATING FIREARM A firearm equipped with a magazine equipped to fire two or more shots.

REVOLVER A repeating firearm which uses a revolving cylinder magazine located between the chamber and the hammer.

RIFLE A firearm with spiral grooves cut in the inside of the barrel. The grooves impart a spin to the projectile to give it greater stability in flight and accuracy.

RIFLED SLUG A lead projectile with rifled grooves cut in its exterior. Designed for use in hunting big game with a shotgun.

RIM FIRE A system of ignition in which the priming mixture is located in the rim of a cartridge. When this rim is struck by the firing pin, it is compressed, setting off the charge.

SAFETY A mechanical device used to prevent accidental discharge of a firearm.

SEAR A lever or series of levers used to assist in transmitting trigger action to the hammer of a gun.

SEMI-AUTOMATIC See autoloader.

SHOT The small pellets loaded in a shotgun shell used to break targets or knock down game.

SHOTGUN A firearm designed to fire shot.

SHOTGUN SHELL A cartridge made with a metal head and a plastic or paper body into which shot is loaded.

SIDE-BY-SIDE A double-barrelled shotgun in which the barrels are located one beside the other on a horizontal plane.

SKEET SHOOTING A clay target shotgun game in which shooting stations are located on a semicircle between two trap houses.

SKEET GUN A shotgun used for skeet shooting.

SLIDE ACTION See pump action.

SMOKELESS POWDER A propellant which burns with very little ash and smoke.

SMOOTH BORE A firearm with no rifling in the barrel. A shotgun.

STOCK The rear part of a firearm, usually wood, used to hold it either in the hand or in position against the shoulder.

TARGET LOAD A shotgun shell used for target shooting.

TRAJECTORY The path of flight of a bullet or projectile.

TRAP A spring-actuated, mechanical device used to throw clay targets.

TRAP GUN A shotgun used for trap shooting.

TRAP SHOOTING A clay-target shotgun game, in which shooting stations are located behind a single trap house.

TRIGGER A finger-actuated lever, located below the receiver, used to release the firing mechanism on a gun.

WADS Spacers used between shot and powder and in the base of shotgun shells.

Index

Numbers in *italic* refer to photographs.